, Nicaragua, on 12 May 1924. ... cons[ ] ean as, since her childhood, she has lived in [ ] dor. She graduated in philosophy and letters from [ ] ington University, Washington DC. She is married to the North American writer Darwin J. Flakoll. They have four children.

For over thirty years, she has been an outstanding force in Central American women's literature. Alone, she has published a dozen volumes of poetry, one of children's stories and two novels. Together with her husband, D.J. Flakoll, she has additionally published two anthologies (of North American poetry and of a hundred of Robert Graves' poems, in translation); two more novels (one still in print by the Salvadorean Ministry of Education, although most of her books are banned there); an historical essay on *El Salvador at the Crossroads* (1980) and *The Sandinista Revolution: a political chronicle of Nicaragua 1855–1979* (1982).

Claribel Alegría and D.J. Flakoll are responsible for bringing Latin American literature (Benedetti, Asturias) to an English-speaking audience, and for translating Morris West and Robert Graves into Spanish. They have lived in many countries in Europe and the Americas, and now divide their time between those continents, lecturing on poetry and the political situation in Nicaragua and El Salvador, and writing a new book on US intervention in the region.

Amanda Hopkinson

Amanda Hopkinson, writer and journalist, was born in London in 1948. She has been involved in the Women's Liberation Movement since 1968. She has lived and travelled extensively in Central America. She has four children and now lives in London. Her first book, a biography of photographer Julia Margaret Cameron, was published in 1986; she is currently editing an anthology of Central American women's poetry to be published by The Women's Press.

CLARIBEL ALEGRÍA

They Won't Take Me Alive

Salvadorean Women in Struggle for National Liberation

Translated by Amanda Hopkinson

 The Women's Press

First published in English by
The Women's Press Limited
A member of the Namara Group
34 Great Sutton Street, London EC1V 0DX

First published as *No Me Agarran Viva* by Claribel Alegría
Copyright © Ediciones Era, S.A. 1983
Translation, Preface and Introduction copyright © Amanda
Hopkinson 1987

British Library Cataloguing in Publication Data

Alegría, Claribel
  They won't take me alive.
  1. El Salvador —— History —— 1944–1979
  2. El Salvador —— History —— 1979–
  I. Title
  972. 84′052   F1488

  ISBN 0-7043-4028-3

Phototypeset in Great Britain by AKM Associates (UK) Ltd
Ajmal House, Hayes Road, Southall, London
Reproduced, printed and bound in Great Britain by
Hazell, Watson and Viney, Aylesbury, Bucks.

For Ana Patricia

Contents

Historical Introduction

One date in the twentieth century stands out as the culmination of El Salvador's history, and the inauguration of a changed perspective. On 22 January 1932 peasants in the west of the country rose in revolt against their cruelly exploitative oligarchic and military overlords. They received variable support from the Communist Party which had initially called for the revolt but which, because of internal disorganisation and penetration by President Martínez' spy network, was unable to provide adequate leadership. In the event, peasant machetes were of little effect against army machine-guns, and assaults on garrisons and military head-quarters were doomed. Within 48 hours, the uprising was put down, with such bloody force that an estimated 30,000 peasants were massacred, compared with fewer than 70 soldiers killed by the insurgents.

The ideological legacy of these events is such that the notorious 'Fourteen Families' who pride themselves on owning El Salvador (and, incidentally, nearly all the media outlets), still successfully disseminate a vitriolic image of 'Communist hordes' about to overrun the country against whom any and every tactic is *a priori* justified. Conversely, on the part of the trade-union and labour movement and the peasantry in general, there is a deep-rooted mistrust of the military in whatever guise they appear. This extends, with considerable historical justification, to a profound suspicion of even 'civilian' government officials who go about with the 'protection' of military escorts, for it goes without saying that the protection is not 'for' but only 'from' the people. An early book by Claribel Alegría, *Cenizas de Izalco* (*Ashes from Izalco*), describes the uprising that occurred when she was a young child. She tells the story of a peasant brought in for questioning by an army commander. When Alegría's father, a doctor, saw the man brutally assaulted, he lost his temper with the commander for employing arms against the unarmed. The commander's response? to assault the doctor.

Violence is endemic in El Salvador, as in so many colonised countries, and dates from the imposition of Spanish rule upon the Pipil, Lenca and Mayan-related tribes of Indians. According to these, the first inhabitants originated from the time when maize was given as a gift from the gods and stored beneath mountains of rock. Since it was a sacred plant, repository of the mould of life (some tribes believing the first man and woman were made from maize mixed with water), it was so well concealed that only the ants, who could carry its small grains on their backs, knew the hiding place. People learned the secret from the ants, but were too big to burrow among the rocks. The help of Tlaloc, the rain god, was invoked to send a storm and wash the stones away; likewise without success. Finally, the elder of the gods collaborated with the woodpecker, who sounded out the rocks to find their weakest spot, then called in the god to blast them apart with thunder. Thus, with the 'food of the gods', the secret of procreation was discovered for which appeasement and offering had to be made at every stage of the crop's cycle of cultivation.

This mythological stage of history, in which 'private and individual ownership of the land was as meaningless as private ownership of the sky, the weather or the sea',[1] reaches back to an unspecified time possibly hundreds of years before the birth of Christ. Certainly, the land had been tilled and populated intensively for several centuries before the Spanish conquest, probably by communities of inter-related Indians who used rather than owned the land

---

[1] David Browning, *El Salvador: Landscape and Society* (Oxford, 1971) p. 16.

belonging to a hierarchy of statesmanlike and priestly elders.

It took from 1522 to 1539 for the Spaniards to subordinate the Indian tribes, their 'pacification' involving also their incorporation into 'Christian civilisation' – inevitably at the bottom of the heap. For the Indians it was a choice between being defined as 'animals' (Spain's view) or slaves (the Church's view). As early as 1528 the first salaried priest arrived from the Spanish mainland, following in the steps of the Franciscan and Dominican friars who saw the Indians, the hispanicised native *ladinos*' and the mixed-race *mestizos*, as 'docile and ready to serve . . . poor wards in need of protection'. It is interesting to note that, during the upheavals of the last six or seven years, it is again the Church which has been brought in as trouble-shooter between government and guerrilla or, as the present Archbishop Rivera y Damas puts it, 'to try and protect the poor and raise consciousness of the issue of human rights and its abuse'.

The sixteenth century saw the Indians principally exploited by their incorporation into a land-system favouring the three main export crops of cocoa, balsam and indigo. The cocoa-producers were mainly independent Pipiles in the Los Izalcos region who sold directly to Spanish traders, the Pipiles being the last tribe to retain an autonomous base in the Cumbre mountains. It was nearer the Pacific port of Acajutla, in Sonsonate, that balsam was produced from tree sap, for use as a herbal remedy and as chrism, used by the Church in anointing. The crop which overtook both of these was the blue dye, indigo, produced from leaves under the most appalling conditions by an Indian workforce. The conditions of its production were so unhealthy that by 1563 the Spanish authorities, concerned at the number of deaths and pulmonary diseases caused by the fumes, prohibited the employment of Indians in the manufacturing process unless they 'volunteered'. Like many laws passed in Castille on behalf of far-distant colonies, this was both humanitarian in intent and unenforceable in practice.

Apart from the demographic disaster – some estimates conclude that El Salvador's population fell from around 120,000 at conquest to 55,000 by 1551 – and the necessity of introducing Black slaves, the indigo estates led to a drastic overthrow of traditional methods of agriculture. Along with cattle-ranching (both cattle and chickens were introduced by the Spaniards, the ranches being created in regions slashed-and-burned by Indians), the estates inaugurated the *hacienda* economy. These were agricultural–pastoral mixed farms, at once self-sufficient in a variety of foodstuffs and tied into the export market through hides and dye. The Indians working them were virtual slaves (though not as completely as the minority of Africans who were specifically excluded from every Spanish edict ordering that the Indians be set free), surviving on the small amount of food they were allowed to grow and take for themselves. The Indians outside the *haciendas* fared no better, since the cattle-land was unfenced and the beasts left to roam throughout their crops and consume much-needed water during the dry season (October to April). Because Indian communities never sought to contain their land, the *hacendado* arrogated to himself the right to use and abuse it.

During the sixteenth century it was less the Indians than the English whom the Spanish settlers feared. By and large, most Indians were regarded as passive and docile, and since they were not equipped to fight conquistadors armed with swords and on horseback, many lost the will to live. While much of this was forced on them by inhumane conditions of labour, there was a measure of choice over the decision not to breed 'more children to suffer and weep as we have had to' as one lament says, and the birth-rate dropped dramatically even where Indians were better used in domestic service. The English, however, under the command of Francis Drake, had harried the Pacific coast intermittently since seizing Jamaica as their regional base in 1568, making the port of Acajutla unsafe as the main export outlet. But despite various pirate incursions by the English over the next two centuries, the British presence seriously re-emerged only through financial investment in the nineteenth century.

By the mid-eighteenth century, indigo had long over-taken cocoa and balsam as the principal export crop, for reasons (as usual) well beyond the control of the growers. Rivalry between El Salvador and neighbouring Guatemala produced, in 1730, an edict prohibiting commerce in cocoa outside the captaincy-general of Guatemala; the imposition of prohibitive taxes on each cocoa-grove dealt the death-blow. Yet political penalties only added to natural devastation, for in 1722 the new volcano of Izalco erupted, destroying the heart of the cocoa-lands and covering surrounding plantations with ash. Although the Indians were commanded to replant, there was an instinctive reluctance to tempt fate once more, and few groves were re-established before imperial favouritism forced Salvador out of the market.

There were other ways in which El Salvador remained a poor relation among the Spanish colonies. By 1770, at a time when Guatemala City and León (the old capital of Nicaragua) boasted universities renowned for their Chairs of Natural and Exact Sciences, there was not even one school in the capital city of San Salvador. Izalco was the centre of education with perhaps as many as 100 enrolled school-pupils, and 100 to 150 more attended school throughout the rest of the entire country. Nor was there a single newspaper, still less a library of any distinction, throughout the colonial period, for literacy was a rare exception, and non-existent among the Indians.

The Indians themselves, although technically permitted to use up to a half of the land for subsistence farming, were burdened with having to pay taxes to Spain, to the Church, to the powerful merchants who controlled all the northern trade-routes of Honduras and Guatemala, and to their local overlords. After 1700 the irregular appropriation of land by the Spanish settlers as a systematic means of effective takeover was resolved by the creation of land titles, primarily to protect the *hacendados*. Possession being, as ever, nine-tenths of the law, the Indians had difficulty proving their ownership of their unfenced communal plots, still less their entitlement to earlier landholdings of which they had been dispossessed by the cattle-ranchers. By 1770 the most important land titles had been granted to a mere 440 *haciendas* and by the close of the colonial period Spaniards controlled as much as one-third of the colony.

The struggle over land divided along caste as well as class lines. The *criollos*, native-born but hispanicised by education and social position, sought to defend their measure of political power through identification with the peninsular Spaniards on whom grace and favour depended. However during the nineteenth century the tables gradually turned and through their employment as *hacendados* and *rancheros* and through administration of local affairs, they eventually turned on their mainland overlords – but in order only to wrest political control for themselves and without making common cause with the dispossessed.

The dispossessed included an uneasy and often only temporary alliance of those of mixed race with the Indians, for whom much of the superstructure of party political battles was irrelevant. At this official level, El Salvador was, during the early nineteenth century, becoming increasingly isolated through its support of a Central American Federation. By 1840 El Salvador was the only state still acknowledging the Federal President Morazán; Guatemala was in the process of electing its own Conservative president; and El Salvador found autonomy forced upon her.

Gradually the precedent became established whereby the army and not the ballot box determined the form of political power. Even on occasions where ballot-boxes have been employed – as, most recently, on four instances between 1981 and 1985 – votes have been elicited and counted at gunpoint, and 'democracy' has been little more than a mandate for dictatorship. After nearly two centuries of blatantly fraudulent elections, there are those who still argue that 'the system [of "military force"] may be said to have reflected popular will comparatively well'.[1]

The mass of the population were by definition of race excluded from the party political process – the continual alternation between Liberal and Conservative administrations – but had a common cause defined through their dispossession of land. The indignation of the Indians against those in the caste immediately above them, the *ladinos*, needed only to be lit by the spark of a final specific injustice.

---

[1] Alaistair White, *El Salvador Nation of the Modern World* (London, 1973) p. 67.

Their simmering resentment over the usurpation of their common lands erupted in 1814, when a parish priest at Los Nonualcos disclosed that local overlords were still exacting a tribute that had in fact been abolished by the Cadiz Parliament. The rebellion appears to have been both spontaneous and leaderless, and consisted of a mass deputation to the town hall at Zacatecoluca which demanded that the tribute be instantly refunded, on pain of the mayor's death. The Indians were reportedly beaten back by a formidable crowd of *ladinos* armed with knives and stones, apparently led by the market women.

In 1833, a similar incident again sparked deep-seated outrage at the misuse of the protective laws of the Spanish Crown by unscrupulous *ladino* parvenus. Blas Aquino, an indigo worker on a *hacienda* also in Los Nonualcos, was placed in public stocks for a misdemeanour over which he protested his innocence. The stocks were in any event illegal, as was the forced labour to which the peons were subjected. Blas' brother, Anastasio, led the uprising in protest at the injustice not only of forced labour but also of press-ganging into the army. In addition to Blas' humiliation there was, during two terrifying days on 3 and 4 January 1833, an unprovoked attack by *ladinos* on the Indian-manned garrison at San Miguel resulting in the massacre of nearly all 100 soldiers. Small wonder that the Indians felt doubly abused: pressed into the army to fight wars on the *ladinos'* behalf in the first place, then slaughtered for their pains when tensions began to run high.

The first act of the ensuing insurrection was to attack the escorts assigned to newly press-ganged Indians, seizing weapons and liberating their fellows. These in turn joined their liberators and, once ranks had swelled to 100-strong, assaults were launched on army posts and thus a force was built which took on government troops. What was perhaps most unusual was that fresh support was recruited on class rather than caste lines, many *ladinos* (themselves also victims of forcible conscription) also joining up. Estates belonging to the wealthy *criollos*, and even the richer *ladinos*, were systematically sacked, with an impressive account made of the goods confiscated to be redistributed among the poor.

This degree of discipline and conscientiousness, so at variance with conquistador conduct, again comes to the fore during the 1932 uprising.

Draconian internal discipline remained in force within the rebel ranks, in the form of decrees demanding major or minor physical amputations for differing degrees of misdemeanour – including the severing of an ear for the crime of wife-beating. Military tactics, however, were not as thoroughly thought through as internal discipline, and the rebel troops failed to capitalise on their main strength – the element of surprise – and march on the capital while government forces were not yet concentrated against them. Instead they dispersed to attack the regional centres of Zacatecoluca and San Vicente, allowing the government time to regroup and muster an offensive that finally routed the rebels on 28 February. Shortly afterwards, parties of Indians from the Guatemalan *altiplano* made their belated arrival to volunteer for the rebel forces, such was the propaganda effect of the 'rising of the dispossessed' and such the trans-national sense of Indian solidarity.[1] Unfortunately, the Guatamalan Indians arrived not to join in Aquino's final push to victory, but to see his head publicly displayed in a cage by the authorities bent on proving their inherent superiority over the 'primitive savages'.

Meanwhile on an economic front, throughout the nineteenth century British and United States' commercial interests were being advanced even when political adventurism failed. Advertisements were placed in the national press to attract European colonisers and boost the exports (and, intermittently, the military command) of most Latin American countries. The diplomatic recognition of the Central American Federation in 1825 brought an influx of predominantly British, Dutch, German and North American

---

[1] There was another example of internationalist 'grapevine solidarity' in 1824, when the short-lived Central American Federation abolished slavery. At that time, there were a mere 1000 slaves left in El Salvador, but many more in neighbouring Guatemala, and these ex-slaves joined together to afford sanctuary to runaway slaves from British-owned Belize in the north, where Blacks were still enslaved.

investors and settlers. Nearly all the infamous 'Fourteen Families' who control so much of El Salvador's wealth today arrived from Europe in the last century and, unlike their counterparts in many adjacent countries, followed in Spanish tradition and assimilated with the local population.

The plan was to advance agri-business and export trading through an aggressive sales policy and the creation of a technological infrastructure to sustain it. The construction of a British communications network in the early decades of this century was but one response to a need that developed out of the agricultural revolution of the last, with El Salvador's transformation into a 'coffee economy'.

Already in the early 1800s coffee was being planted on the highlands but sold at an even higher price than its retail value in Europe. Since Europe was the traditional trade outlet, there was clearly no market for such an expensive product, particularly given the significance of it as a Costa Rican and Brazilian export. But in 1840 a Brazilian entrepreneur named Coelho introduced other methods of crop-cultivation; coffee became suddenly economically viable and began to subordinate traditional products in the country's economy. Within the decade, the Salvadorean government was not merely providing incentives to growers through the distribution of land and free coffee saplings, but even fining or imprisoning farmers reluctant to change their ways. By the 1870s the rise of coffee was further hastened by the collapse of the indigo market, when a substitute synthetic blue dye was invented in Germany.

The British contribution was to sustain and enhance the new *cafetalera* oligarchy by means of substantial investment in the railways, mines and canal routes. Since 1824, when Britain had touted for a commission to build a first Central American canal, El Salvador was placed in the midst of continually renegotiated foreign loans and an international debt from which the country has never been able to extricate itself. The United States rapidly joined the investment scramble, initially also tendering for the canal project, but later generating private companies concerned with paving the streets and providing electricity and also introducing the benefits of insurance investment and diversification of commerce to boost exports of cotton, timber, cotton and henequen.

It was through business practices and commercial interventions such as these that Western economic imperialism began to take over where Spanish colonial imperialism had left off. By determining internal development and external export markets, the United States increasingly gained control over a tiny piece of land that would come to be seen as of strategic necessity. Or, as Reagan calls it with chilling quaintness, 'just a bit of my back yard'.

The immediate context in which the 1932 rebellion arose was geographical as much as economic and political, and in every sense linked to the sudden ascendency of coffee as a crop that monopolised vast stretches of the western region. At a suitable altitude it covered so much of the ground that there was no room for the local population to grow any of their own crops, leaving them entirely dependent on seasonal labour for their livelihood. In 1931, the coffee export price suddenly dropped to 18 *colones* a *quintal* (46 kilos) as against 39 *colones* in 1928, and the fall was immediately passed on to the workers, some of whom found their wages slashed from 75 to 25 *centavos* overnight. To add insult to injury, the allowance of beans and rice on which those robbed of their land and any measure of self-sufficiency were dependent, was also withdrawn by some landowners, forcing many families whose subsistence was already precarious directly into starvation.

No such crisis prevailed anywhere east of Lake Ilopango, so there was no revolt even in the traditionally militant area of Nonualco, where crops were diversified and smallholdings persisted. Even in the western zone, there were other factors that turned areas of potential insurrection away from hostility born of desperation. Generally, where the coffee-planters still resided on their estates rather than in the capital, and were better acquainted and concerned with their pickers' lot and thus more willing to fight wage-cutting, the pickers resisted joining the rebellion. It was true that, even in the hottest moments of the uprising, the mansions of the rare 'good masters' were spared the attacks and sacking awarded to the rest.

The revolt was not an entirely rural phenomenon. In 1927 Pío Romero Bosque had been elected President in the freest elections in Salvadorean history and opened up political discussion on questions of economic redistribution and the reduction of privilege. In 1928 he decreed tax exemption for income derived from cereal and pulse cultivation. This apparent bias towards the popular forces led to the formation, the following year, of an employers' clique called the Society for the Defence of Coffee, a cartel that still seeks to direct government policy today. In 1930 the Communist Party was founded at a secret meeting in a wood near Lake Ilopango, and at once pledged to fight increasing United States' involvement in El Salvador[1] and to defend the declining living standards of both urban and rural workers.

That year Don Pío was peacefully succeeded in the presidency by Arturo Araujo, a man drawn from the landowning élite who had received part of his education in England, where he lived in the home of a Liverpool shop steward and met his English wife, Dora. His party was named the *Partido Laborista Salvadoreño* in clear deference to the British Labour Party, and at first he incorporated some working-class reforms in his election campaign. One of his first acts on assuming the presidency, however, was to reassure his aristocratic colleagues by imprisoning Agustín Farabundo Martí, the popular communist leader.

Before the beginning of December 1931, when new elections were again being called, Araujo both permitted the Communist Party to participate (something that has not happened before or since), and denounced the social-reform plans of its leaders as 'fanatical'. Meanwhile, the revolutionaries were setting up unions and pulling out workers to attend demonstrations against conditions of labour. Some 80,000 coffee-pickers in the west were unionised and in the capital strikes were followed up with mass marches. The

---

[1] United States' intervention in Nicaragua, which put the Salvadorean upper-class on their mettle lest their own country should be next, was an important factor deciding Claribel Alegría's father to move to El Salvador.

army used the unrest as a pretext to precipitate a coup, overthrowing Araujo on 2 December and installing themselves in a position of power they would refuse to vacate until the nominal change to civilian government with Duarte's election in 1981.

At first the army, under General Maximiliano Hernández Martínez, delayed imposing outright repression. Revolutionary newspapers could continue publication and the Communist Party was allowed to participate in municipal elections. However, no sooner had communists won seats in western towns than they were forbidden to take office. This proved the last straw for the revolutionary leaders, who none the less lacked the co-ordination necessary to launch an immediate popular response. Twice the planned uprising was postponed, giving government forces time to seize Farabundo Martí and two student comrades, with the result that their fellow-leaders sought to call the whole thing off. Communications were so bad, however, that no systematic contact was made with outlying regional centres and in some areas the rebellion went off at half-cock.

It is always easy to be judgmental in retrospect, in this instance both about the immediate causes of the revolt and about its subsequent management. Yet there can be little doubt that the insurrection occurred in response to expectations falsely raised on the one hand by a short-lived reformist government and on the other by a youthfully zealous Communist leadership, which were later crushed to a level of despair when the self-styled leadership proved ineffective.

The shock-waves that rippled through the ruling oligarchy at the temerity of rebellion seem particularly inappropriate when contrasted with the repeated expressions of surprise that little of this kind had previously occurred in the whole sorry history of El Salvador's battle for the land and its fertile riches. A number of contemporary, often right-wing, sources describe the country as so 'ripe for Communism' that the ruling oligarchy could be toppled at any moment. In December 1931, a US military attaché accurately predicted the effects of a situation in which 'roughly 90 per cent of the wealth of the nation is held by about half of 1 per cent of the

12

population. Thirty or forty families own nearly everything in the country. They live in almost regal style . . . the rest of the population has practically nothing.'[1]

And with the wisdom of hindsight the Canadian Naval Commander V.G. Brodeur explained:

> The revolution was entirely due to lack of consideration for the Indians. There are only two classes in El Salvador, i.e. the very rich and the Indians. The very rich are very few and it is noticeable that these left the country the minute the trouble started . . . From observation, it is doubtful if the Indians who took part in the revolution knew what bolshevism meant. To them it meant an organisation to release them from slavery.

As in the earlier revolts of the nineteenth century, the rebels again made and abided by their own rules. In contrast to press allegations that 'atheist Communist hordes' were sacking and pillaging churches, careful exception was made not only of churches and chapels but also of roadside and family shrines. Even the palatial residences of wealthy landowners were spared if their residents had the reputation of showing any concern for their workforce. It was undoubtedly the absentee landlords, who ruled through cruel managers, whose property was most fiercely attacked.

The uprising of machetes was answered by the full firepower of a heavily equipped army. They attacked an ill-defined consortium of 30,000 urban trade unionists, members of political opposition parties and a vastly greater number of peasants, largely women and children, who had nothing whatever to do with the revolt. The revenge was so horrific that even its perpetrators began to have their doubts. A trade-union leader who survived the firing squad later recalled:

> From the barracks at Ahuachapán a stream of blood flowed, as if it were water, or horses' urine . . . the peasants who were being

---

[1] The following quotations are included in Michael McClintock's excellent volume, *The American Connection* (London 1985), pp. 99–103.

shot in the patio would sing 'Sacred Heart, You will Reign' [a Catholic hymn] and (a lieutenant reported) in the pools of blood he and the soldiers in the firing squad had seen, clear as can be, the image of Christ and had refused to go on killing and protested to their superiors.[1]

In the countryside thatched huts were set on fire and the inhabitants mown down with machine-gun fire as they fled; sometimes the entire population of a village was lined up against a church wall (often the only stone building) and shot at 'until the wall looked like lace'; sometimes, after racking peasant encampments with machine-gun fire, survivors were lined up and 'The males over 10 or 12 were shot, with or without prior torture, with or without interrogation . . . When there were no survivors, they would put the cadavers in the fork of a tree, or on a stake, and hang signs on them warning that this was the fate that awaited all communists.'

The peasants were hunted down not only in the region of the revolt, but on the basis simply of their dress or 'caste of features'. It is from 1932 that the ending of an indigenous style of dressing, language and traditions most clearly dates, and it became a crime to be a native Salvadorean. In the cities, the search for communists had a more political than a racial bias: anyone who was not in favour of the power of the oligarchy and the security forces was a communist. The paranoia against trade unionists, in the early stages of the movement often petty businessmen and craftsmen, was so extreme that when 100 anti-communist guild members volunteered to help a garrison in San Salvador they were shot dead in the courtyard of the barracks out of sheer paranoia.

Perhaps the cruellest irony is that, not being guilty of the crimes of, which they were accused in the first place, the Indians were so viciously repaid in what was bruited to be their own currency. In 1971 the professedly neutral United States historian Thomas Anderson investigated the tales of

---

[1] Michael McClintock *op. cit.*, pp. 99–103.

revolutionary arson, rape and murder and was unable to verify them. Even his estimate of probably six civilian (and not above 30) deaths at the hands of the 1932 rebels is denied by the few surviving leaders. It is not only the case that common Indian tradition is life-respecting and 'seeks the gentle way', but that in the towns that were successfully captured and briefly held (Izalco, Sonsonate, Nahuizalco, Juayua and Tacuba), the inhabitants were impressed that the aggression was so specifically directed at the military – all the braver, in view of the almost complete lack of fire-arms among the insurrectionaries.

The impact of this legacy of carnage continues in its mythmaking power. Certainly, stereotypes are firmly implanted in the descendents of the opposing sides: the peasantry see the armed forces (whether military or paramilitary, secret, security or Treasury police) as essentially there to protect and further the interests of an entrenched oligarchy at any cost. And the peasantry themselves are viewed with hostile suspicion as permanently either on the brink of open revolt, or as secretly colluding with 'sworn revolutionaries'. The real horror, however, is that the army still continues to behave much as it did in 1932, only equipped with all the sophisticated weaponry another half-century of United States' technology (and money) can buy.

If the repression hasn't ceased, then neither have the social causes that give rise to an incipient state of insurrection. In June 1983 a checklist compiled for the University of Central America's publishing house enumerated such facts as:

1. Population density is 200 per square kilometre, and in San Salvador over 200,000 people(nearly 25 per cent) live in subhuman conditions – with cardboard or newspaper covering, no plumbing facilities, running water or electricity.

2. Less than half of 1 per cent of the owners possess 37.3 per cent of the arable land while 91.4 per cent own just 21.9 per cent.

3. Just 16 per cent of the economically active population work all the year round.

4. 60 per cent of the Salvadoreans living in rural areas and 40 per cent of those living in the cities cannot read or write.

15

5. There are under two hospital beds per 10,000 inhabitants while there are no reliable infant mortality data (in San Salvador the Demographical Association gives a figure of 48 per 100,000; England's figure is 13), but in the countryside few sick people have ever seen a doctor and are mainly attended by midwives and nurses within their community or, occasionally, a visiting district nurse from a regional centre.

6. There are less than three doctors per 10,000 inhabitants and most of the country's 1,300 doctors are concentrated in the capital.

One of Duarte's more recent moves, in the spring of 1986, has been to more than halve a hospital doctor's salary from a mere 700 *colones* to 300 (or 70 dollars) a month as part of the enormously unpopular 'economic package'. Doctors therefore, along with many other mobile white-collar workers, are following in the footsteps of so many of the rising generation of *cafetaleros* and entering voluntary exile in the United States. There are communities of fellow-Salvadorean exiles to employ their skills – reputedly 80,000 strong in Washington, an astonishing 350,000 in California. And while doctors increasingly join the drain of professionals out of a country that desperately needs them, the US government has just voted further 'aid' of 500 million dollars for the next financial year that will predominantly go towards disappropriating, maiming or killing more of a people desperately in need of minimum provision to stay alive.

According to another, more recent, university report – that of José Simeón Cañas – Salvador has now a 'hunger economy'. Its projection is that if the hunger (i.e. war) economy ended today, it would take until 2010 to return the country even to the low standard of living it enjoyed when military rule formally ended in 1979. The dearth of a professional class; the lack of institutions of learning, health and welfare; the collapse of a whole infrastructure of communications, building, transport, etc.; the creation of a whole generation of physically and/or psychologically damaged children; and the repeated hike in the fixed price of basic foodstuffs (most recently, in April 1986, of 50 to 75 per cent) imply a country in need of fundamental and prolonged reconstruction.

Where years of military terror have had erratic application

in the countryside, recent systematic bombing has been deployed to clear whole zones under guerrilla control. Aside from the directly human cost, this has the additional effect of further distorting land-distribution. Even in 1985, before the recent 'clean sweep' operations, nearly half of El Salvador's population was landless and 90 per cent of tenures were so small that no family could subsist on them. Land ownership was concentrated so that 2 per cent of the population owned over 60 per cent of the cultivable ground. The lack of an alternative to some degree of self-sufficiency is underlined by the fact that half the national income is awarded to a mere 8 per cent of the population, leaving 58 per cent earning under 10 dollars a month and over 80 per cent earning less than 20 dollars. As peasants dispossessed of their land are obliged to become dependent on waged labour, so they come up against some of the highest rates of under- and un-employment in the Americas. Due to the seasonal character of most forms of employment the majority of rural em-ployees work for a maximum of a half of each working year.

There are still disquieting similarities between the condi-tions in the 1930s and those 50 years later. The trail blazed in the first decades of this century by Western countries seeking investment outlets has continued, with haphazard develop-ment of 'services' based on profit rather than need. At the time of writing, nearly half San Salvador's inhabitants live in cardboard or plastic shacks, without water, electricity or sewage and rubbish disposal. Almost none of these slums have paved access and are thrown up under the flyovers of main roads, along waterways that turn into open sewers, in the interstices of some of the capital's most central or middle-class neighbourhoods. In the countryside, domestic life has few amenities. Homes are primitive, made from a 'cement' formed from dust and water used to fill parallel 'walls' of woven laths or reeds. Where water is scarce (and the water table has dropped drastically in areas where the army's 'scorched earth' policy has eradicated water-retaining ground cover) polluted water is resorted to, and it is not un-common to encounter groups of villagers using stagnant river and lake-edges for toilet, washing and drinking purposes.

Whereas El Salvador suffers the same demographic

problem as many Third World countries, with over one-third of its tiny population clustered in and around the capital, the last half century has seen a paradoxical strengthening of ties between those remaining in the countryside. A process that began when *indio* and poor *ladino* made common cause in the nineteenth century has given way to a stage where the two groups are synonymously referred to as *campesino*, usually a peasant small-holder but sometimes also a waged agricultural labourer. Indians as a distinct group vanished after 1932: hounded for any vestiges of clothing, custom or physical feature that might mark them out as 'savages', they had to shed their distinguishing characteristics in order to survive at all. Names, clothes and habits were changed, native languages and traditions suppressed, and today there is a striking contrast between the Salvadorean Indians, only distinguishable by race, and those in neighbouring Guatemala, with their brilliant costumes and wealth of indigenous cultures.

This cultural genocide waged by the authorities accelerated a process of assimilation that was already well under way. The cruelty of the fact that the military now in no way differentiate between the civilians they persecute means an identity of suffering between all those left in the scourged areas. In those under guerrilla control, an estimated number of up to some 300,000 people enjoy a lifestyle and sense of dignity denied by the appalling national statistics of military killings and social and educational deprivation. And in May 1986 there were again signs of an insistence upon the need to break the military deadlock and force a so-called 'civilian' and 'Christian' government to assume responsibility. A woman guerrilla commander with the FDR-FMLN, cast in the mould of Eugenia, spoke not only of the inevitable 'prolonged popular war' but also of insistence upon dialogue, that the government return to the negotiating table, as they did for the recent talks mediated by Alan García, President of Peru.

The April bombings of Arcatao, and the army's imprisonment of the survivors in a nearby church until, starving, they were forced to sacrifice some of their young men, is yet another tactic the government cannot defend, and is under increasing international pressure to do so. At a May Day demonstration, attended by a number of Democratic

Congressmen from the United States and human rights observers, 100,000 Salvadoreans took to the streets with their union and party banners. The military filmed and then pulled in individuals for questioning, but there was none of the concerted violence which characterised the ambush and attack launched against the major demonstration of 1980.

At that time the FMLN found itself to be 'a vanguard without an army'. Now it is optimistic that it is armed and ready, though choosing to deploy its forces in defence of the people within the controlled zones. The grassroots desire for peace and change is manifest in the number of people now prepared to take to the streets in one-day stoppages protesting that 'Duarte's democracy is fancy-dress' and demanding that he fulfil his promises. While the death squads have made an unwelcome return to city streets, Duarte has at last felt shamed into instituting some show trials of the most blatant perpetrators of atrocities.

Even the most deprived are starting to organise: 23,000 of an estimated half-million *desplazados* (displaced persons) have formed a union to fight for a return to their homes and compensation for damage done by the armed forces. The military tactic of physically detaching the guerrilla move-ment from its popular base through aerial bombing, mass evacuations and terror, is clearly failing. The peasants repeatedly point to a brutal army to explain their plight, as the industrial and agricultural workers point to an inept and impotent government. The chilling military suggestion that 'If we could afford to lose 30,000 in 1932, we can lose another 250,000 now'[1] is a bankrupt response to a problem that won't go away. As a spokesperson for the Salvadorean Trade Union Congress (UNTS) explained to me: 'Our May Day rally demonstrates the difference between reality and appearance, the popular will and the public image. What we want is peace and genuine democracy, not rule by the United States through the armed forces.'

Amanda Hopkinson, July 1986.

---

[1] See Mario Menendez Rodriguez, *Voices From El Salvador* (San Francisco, 1983) p. 159

Preface

Visting El Salvador in 1986 is still a discomforting experience, even ten years into the armed struggle that is the historical grist of this book. The elementary statistics of El Salvador's grotesque demographic distortions won't go away. Out of a population of only 5 million, one million are now in exile (like Claribel Alegría, the author); half a million more are internal refugees, mostly homeless and destitute; according to the most conservative estimates available, at least 50,000 people have been killed in what has increasingly the appearance of a genocidal civil war, peasants being the principal victims of slaughter at the hands of the army; an average of five deaths daily, through the systematic attempted liquidation of political and popular opposition, as well as unexplained individual 'disappearances'. In the latter instances over 90 per cent of suspects are believed to have been tortured, before being murdered, and the corpses dumped.

Since *They Won't Take Me Alive* was written, some of the tactics of intimidation have changed, but the terror and carnage remain. United States' pressure and an intermittent concern for world opinion have prevented a repetition of the mass killing of students out on a rag-day procession (see page 65); mutilated torsos and severed heads are no longer regularly exhibited along the highway like gory mediaeval 'warnings' (see page 126); six years have elapsed since Archbishop Romero was gunned down before his stunned congregation as he appealed to the soldiers to listen to their consciences as well as to their commanders.

Yet, in the countryside, the recent indiscriminate bombings

sponsored by the United States under the code-name 'Operation Phoenix' have devastated populated areas of the Morazán and Guazapa regions. El Salvador, smaller geographically than Wales, covers only 20,000 square kilometres, and has a higher population density than any other Central American country. With 200 inhabitants to every square kilometre, any major air-strikes are bound to produce civilian casualties. Operation Phoenix is described as a 'cleaning-up procedure', designed to push the Farabundo Martí National Liberation Front (FMLN) back from the boundaries of the zones they control, and to flush out any suspected sympathisers from among the peasantry. A new feature, imported from the United States along with the bombs and planes, is a programme of 'psychological propaganda'. Newspapers willingly disseminate what the armed forces now seek to indoctrinate their prisoners with: that their actions are a regrettable necessity in the face of the 'threat to democracy' posed by the FMLN and FDR, and that the guerrillas are directly responsible for any 'mishaps or excesses'.

The guerrilla-controlled zones which cover roughly a geographical third of the country are indeed a threat to the military government – though their ideology may be no more 'subversive' than a new order of priorities. The familiar slogan 'bread, shelter and work' becomes a guarantee, alongside the commitment to primary healthcare and basic education, all luxuries denied by successive national dictatorships whether personal or military. What cannot, however, be guaranteed are the peace and security that every Salvadorean longs for. The bombs dropped by Operation Phoenix and its successors leave craters ten metres in diameter and not only score direct hits against humans but destroy crops and livestock as well. The air-strikes are in any case followed up by land forces 'sweeping clean', razing fields and houses and forcibly transporting the residents to Red Cross posts. To ensure they cannot return, the whole area is then put to the torch. It was one of the many painfully ironic contradictions between El Salvador's public and internal image that, in March 1986, at the same time as funds for minor reforestation projects had successfully been culled from the EEC, the army was consigning the trees of Guazapa to a bonfire.

Since the government, through blaming the guerrillas, takes no responsibility for dispossessing the peasantry, it not only offers no compensation for the loss of lands and lives, but seeks to sell the destitute peasants new strips of land in neighbouring provinces. For the peasantry a complete inability to pay is compounded by a sense of outrage, as the vast majority find themselves transferred into refugee camps run by the Archdiocese of El Salvador. There, within sight of the smouldering remains of their homes, they are subjected to the further indignities of sporadic military interventions, a few hundred soldiers appearing in the middle of the night to harass the residents and workers on what is designated 'neutral' territory. As one foreign commentator, a North American solicitor working for an international agency, concluded: 'If these people had never had a thought about the guerrilla movement in their heads, they'd have to think about joining up by now. What else is left for them to do? The refugee camps are the best ideological training the guerrilla could have asked for.'

The Salvadorean guerrilla movements share a saying that 'Here the people serve as our mountains'. Guerrilla warfare is supposed to be practicable primarily in mountainous terrain, giving cover for tactics of ambush and withdrawal, sabotage and protection from air-attacks. El Salvador's tiny size and exposed, highly cultivated landscape doesn't automatically lend itself to a traditional guerrilla war in the manner of other Latin American countries. Hence the need to be able to melt into a crowd, to know that cover, anonymity and protection will be willingly given by the people in whose cause the struggle is undertaken.

'Eugenia', the pseudonym of Claribel Alegría's heroine, was led to join the guerrilla wing of the FMLN through a series of steps that began when, as a schoolgirl, she became a Catholic 'missionary' to the city slums and which culminated in her becoming commander of a major division of the Popular Liberation Forces. To visit San Salvador after reading the book is to encounter a city of ghosts. Here is Cuzcatlán Park where the student demonstrators were massacred by the military; the Cathedral is still pocked with bullet holes where the army racked it with rounds of machine-gun fire as people fled for refuge in January 1980; the walls of Avenida Roosevelt are still scrawled with the names of the political and Christian organisations with which Eugenia worked.

The Catholic University where she was a student is still subject to repression: 14 bombs have exploded in its printing presses in attempts to prevent the Jesuits from publishing what no commercial outlet dared (including the international bestseller describing the life of a Chalatenango peasant woman, Manlio Argueta's *One Day of Life*). Despite the intimidation that has caused the exodus of nearly half its staff, and the sporadic murders of both students and lecturers on its campus, its religiously protected status means the Catholic University has suffered less widespread violence than the national one. This was closed down, amid mass shootings, by the army in 1980 and was only partially reopened in 1985 without either the basic infrastructure of an educational establishment or compensation for the estimated 30 million dollars worth of damage caused. In 1986, buildings remain gutted and burnt-out buses litter the grounds; the science labs, libraries and printing press are only gradually being re-established with international assistance; even the desperately needed medical and dental departments lack basic equipment.

On the streets of the capital and on the countryside roads, the army is still an inescapable presence. With 57,000 of the country's tiny population in olive-green or camouflage uniform, perhaps it's not surprising that there are truckloads of soldiers at so many intersections or that the skies are so busy with their helicopters. An armed man guards the entrance to every public building from the post office to a McDonalds hamburger bar. It was in one of these in 1986 that a British photographer was shot by a jumpy security guard, a fitting example of North American money employing the trigger-happy locals. In June 1985, the FMLN took responsibility for the attack on a club in the Zona Rosa, in which nine civilians and four US marines were killed. Since then there has been less of a US-military profile, and even

23

businessmen have been told to 'keep their heads down' – advice that amuses some Salvadoreans who, noting the sudden upsurge in US embassy 'staff', conclude that the lowered heads are being put together inside that ambassadorial fortress.

Certainly, US big business can profit from the continuing exodus of native coffee and cotton barons, spurred on by growing economic sabotage from the guerrillas. Economic aid, which helps both multinationals and private businesses exploit the dearth of Salvadorean commercial infrastructure and a cheap source of labour (the more readily exploited, with unemployment as high as 42 per cent), has taken a sharp upturn, increasing by 94 per cent between 1984–5 to reach 432.22 million dollars. Military aid jumped from a mere 6,200 million dollars in 1980 to 146,250 million dollars in 1985 though this figures represents a drop of 50 million dollars on the previous year. This was partly due to figure-juggling, for example Reagan's repeated requests for 'supplementaries' (the latest of which was 27 million dollars labelled 'anti-terrorist aid'), and partly to do with the achievement of saturation levels of certain types of the most expensive heavy equipment. In the 18 months since Duarte assumed the presidency, the armed forces have grown by over 10 per cent; the helicopter fleet has tripled in size and now has 61 choppers, and gunships and troop transporters; military intelligence has been boosted by considerably more sophisticated ground-to-ground, ground-to-air and air-to-ground communications networks, allowing a more accurate (and so more devastating) deployment of joint army–airforce operations.

Small wonder, then, that the US has been called El Salvador's 'super-government', with Duarte simply in position as a mouthpiece and manager. It is not a job he – or anyone – can accomplish with any degree of conviction or dignity, as he himself pointed out in an interview with *Playboy* magazine, in June 1984:

The aid is given under such conditions that its use is really decided by the Americans and not by us . . . how many planes and helicopters we buy . . . how many trucks we need . . . how many pairs of boots . . . are decided by the one who supplies the money. And all of the money is spent over there. We never see a penny of it, because everything arrives here already paid for.

The list of US manipulators does not stop with the arms manufacturers and suppliers, the military 'advisors' and 'trainers' or even the President. US-AID and the IMF (International Monetary Fund) are also implicated in channelling funds in ways that assist US financial and commercial interests, attempting to coerce the government into reneging on its election pledges of 1984 and 1985, and renouncing any attempt at social reform in favour of shoring up what AID describes as 'a coherent national strategy of investment which will help the private sector take advantage of the opportunities presented by the CBI Caribbean Basin Initiative, restore the activity in "free zones" and, in general take advantage of the qualified and cheap labour force, and its proximity to the United States.'

It has long been convenient for the US to view Costa Rica, since the abolition of its army in 1948, as 'the Switzerland of Central America', a nearby 'neutral' territory from which to mount surveillance operations on neighbouring Nicaragua. El Salvador has extended the European analogy, being cast in the role of Germany, for the famed diligence and aptitude of its workforce. But in terms of the workers' own conditions of labour, there is more similarity with the long hours and low wages of workers in Hong Kong or Taiwan. In *They Won't Take Me Alive* it is no coincidence that when Marina is deemed unemployable by virtue of her political record, it is cheap toys from these countries that she ends up selling on the streets (see page 125). And the circumstances of her job in the Maidenform factory, where she is switched from skilled seamstress to heavy sewing-machinist manufacturing rucksacks for the Vietnam war, chillingly point up the overlap between US investment and military policies throughout the world (see page 119).

Despite this inpouring of US 'aid' to business and military interests, El Salvador has a mounting foreign debt crisis and an acute shortage of all-important dollar currency. Since late 1984, the FMLN have concentrated new effort on economic sabotage to apply still more pressure to the already hard-pressed commercial sector. In the single month of December, sabotage to the coffee estates in the eastern region alone totalled 4.32 million dollars, a serious loss in view of the falling output in major crop production since 1979. A different tactic within the same design is the assertion of control over the country's transport arteries. In 1985 eleven transport stoppages were inflicted by rebel forces, leaving only the eastern section of the country running at all for the 77 working days affected and costing the economy at least 58 million dollars. In 1986, the main north–south routes have been repeatedly paralysed, and all public transport intermittently stopped in the capital. Railway transportation is now virtually impossible, and access to the ports so restricted as to make nonsense of AID/CBI programmes of massive exports.

Within the capital, the main evidence of guerrilla activity is still another form of sabotage: that of the electricity and telephone lines. It is an eerie experience to be in a busy downtown centre at night when there is a sudden blackout that includes all the street lights, leaving only the distant military hospital with its separate generator emitting a dim neon glare. By day, the military hospital is surrounded with uniformed soldiers in wheelchairs and on crutches, many the victims of land-mines planted by the guerrillas which account for at least 25 per cent of army casualties (another recently accelerated FMLN tactic.)

On the streets, the main political focus has switched to the trade unions, with an upsurge in strikes and demonstrations against the war and the government's unpopular 1986 'economic package'. Salaried workers find themselves joining those in the private sector, bearing the brunt of Duarte's vain attempt to mollify two incompatible sets of demands. The IMF has insisted on the devaluation of the national currency while the mixed business sector (of the traditional oligarchy, the North American investors and the petty entrepreneurs) is pressing for better returns. The consumer loses out through rises in prices and public service charges, while the better-organised labour federations (like the teachers' union, ANDES, through which Ana María gained her political education, see pages 111–12) are fighting a serious cut in real wages.

The army weighs in with its determination to maintain the entire country on an indefinite war footing – expressed by Defence Minister Vides Casanova in an uncompromising speech which opened: 'All the resources of the state must be placed at the service of our final victory. Only by completely defeating the enemies of the fatherland can we recover peace and prosperity'. The rebel forces find themselves obliged to conclude, with ERP Commander Joaquín Villalobos, that the military are indeed backed by 'an enemy with an inexhaustible source of material resources'. Both sides have had to refine and adapt their tactics since Eugenia assumed a regional command. The army's increase in covert intelligence-gathering (including the US-designed 'psych-ops', psychological operations to convert the otherwise reluctant peasantry) and in air-power (with its concomittant proven willingness to blast whole civilian-populated regions out of existence, if that means getting at 'guerrilla bases') have made it impossible for the rebel forces to pin down ground battalions in large-scale confrontations where losses were bound to be heavy and military morale consequently low.

None the less, whether one believes the government statistic of 4,000 troops lost or the FMLN version (more than double), the capacity of the guerrillas to inflict heavy losses in the massed offensives of 1982 and '83 was clearly proven. While the army has subsequently sought to undercut that tactic, and has had some success in dismantling the FMLN's supply routes for arms, medicines and food, the rebel units have successfully stepped up the selective ambush of government forces and targeting of military and US officials.

And despite the harassment and exhaustion of a frequently attacked and dispossessed civilian population, Duarte's Christian Democratic representatives have been obliged to acknowledge the loss of several rural areas to rebel control. Mayors have been withdrawn from municipalities in the departments of Usulután, San Miguel, Cabañas and Chalatenango, and an attempt at maintaining even the presence of local government remains only in the departmental capitals. Within the liberated zones, the people have their first experience of a participatory democracy, in which Councils of Popular Power determine the running of daily life in all its aspects, from those of necessary military patrols and defence to basic education and health. The panic Eugenia endured when her daughter was sick with diarrhoea is characteristic of a country where dehydration and malnutrition are killers that eliminate a fifth of Salvadorean children under the age of five, leaving three-quarters of the survivors to linger suffering some degree of malnutrition. As the private sector commercial interests nudge the harder at those of the military, so there is even more of a squeeze upon the Christian Democrats' much-vaunted programme of social welfare and reform, now in indefinite abeyance, and by contrast even more significance is attached to the achievements within the liberated zones.

In addition to the warfare by sabotage and peace-keeping by the parallel government within the FMLN and ERP zones, strategic military and economic targets have been successfully assailed in the five years since Eugenia was killed. What is astonishing in, for example, the assault on the Cerrón Grande dam in 1984 or the Armed Forces Military Training Centre in 1985, is their demonstration of the FMLN's capacity to launch an offensive and withdraw and disperse in such large numbers and in so few hours. Again, without a strong popular base (the people compensating for the lack of mountains once more) such dramatic assaults would be impossible.

It was, however, the kidnap of Duarte's daughter by the FMLN in autumn 1985, and the spectacular concessions the FMLN won for her return, that really pushed the President to one side. Never having been given the option of serving as more than a face-saving device for US military strategy in the region, Duarte, by his capitulation to secure the release of his daughter, is now generally regarded as, at best, finished and, at worst, a lunatic. Or, in the words of one high-ranking officer: 'Duarte might be mad, but he's not stupid. He knows that if he tried to get rid of the security forces, we'll overthrow him.'

A measure of the security forces' recognition that Duarte is merely the US's puppet is seen in their increasing confidence in putting two fingers up to both sides. Duarte's usefulness to the United States resides in his ability to put a civilian veneer on a country steeped in civil war, a veneer worn thin both by his inability to deliver on his election promises of internal reform and redistribution of wealth and by the reappearance of the security forces' least savoury characteristics. Death squads (or 'the army in disguise' as they are known) have made an unwelcome reappearance; political detainees (according to information collated by the Archdiocese's legal section) are routinely subjected to torture in order to secure information and extra-judicial confessions (thus bypassing an already weak legal system); 'disappearances' are again on the increase to add to the figure of more than 4,000 effected by previous régimes and that of 50,000 civilians murdered.

Yet, if there is little indication that the security forces feel seriously curtailed by the presence of a 'civilian' and 'democratic' (still less 'Christian') government, there is the North American conviction that, as one commentator put it: 'The US embassy is there to ensure that the security forces can never simply take over.' Despite the economic force of the United States and the military strength of the army, the revolutionary movements retain a creative ability to adapt and surprise. The mass mobilisations and successful insurrections described in this book solidified into the local democratic governments of the liberated zones. The political struggle in the capital has re-emerged in the new wave of public sector demonstrations and transport and hospital strikes.

What Eugenia and her comrades hoped would be a triumph on a par with those in Cuba and Nicaragua has settled into what the revolutionary movements term a 'prolonged popular war'. Its forms may change to include selective kidnap and economic sabotage, but the ideology remains the same: that of a people fighting for dignity, self-determination and freedom.

Amanda Hopkinson, July 1986

Glossary

ACUS: Acción Católica Universitaria (University Catholic Action)

ANDES: Asociación Nacional de Educadores Salvadoreños (National Association of Salvadorean Educationalists)

BID: Banco Internacional de Desarrollo (International Development Bank)

BPR: Bloque Popular Revolucionario (Popular Revolutionary Bloc, allied with the FPL)

CONDECA: Consejo de Defensa Centroamericana (Central American Defence Council)

CUSS: Confederación Unificada de Sindicalistas Salvadoreñas (United Federation of Salvadorean Trades Unionists)

DRU: Dirección Revolucionaria Unificada (Unified Revolutionary Tendency, of the FMLN)

ERP: Ejército Revolucionario del Pueblo (People's Revolutionary Army)

FAPU: Frente de Acción Popular Unificado (United Popular Action Front)

FDR: Frente Democrático Revolucionario (Revolutionary Democratic Front)

FECCAS: Federación Cristiana de Campesinos Salvadoreños (Christian Federation of Salvadorean Peasants)

FMLN: Frente Farabundo Martí para la Liberación Nacional (Farabundo Martí National Liberation Front)

FPL: Fuerzas Populares de Liberación Farabundo Martí (Farabundo Martí Popular Liberation Forces)

FSLN: Frente Sandinista de Liberación Nacional (Sandinista National Liberation Front, of Nicaragua)

FTC: Federación de Trabajadores del Campo (Federation of

Rural Workers, a union of UTC and FECCAS)

JEC: Juventud de Estudiantes Cristianos (Christian Student Youth Movement)

MCCA: Mercado Común Centroamericano (Central American Common Market)

MNR: Movimiento Nacional Revolucionario (National Revolutionary Movement, the social democrats)

MUS: Movimiento Universitario Socialista (University Socialist Movement)

ORDEN: Organisación Democrática Nacionalista (Democratic Nationalist Organisation, paramilitary)

PCN: Partido de Conciliación Nacional (Party of National Conciliation, an official party)

PCS: Partido Comunista Salvadoreño (Salvadorean Communist Party)

PDC: Partido Demócrata Cristiano (Christian Democratic Party)

PRN: Partido de Reconciliación Nacional (Party of National Reconciliation, official)

UDN: Unión Democrática Nacional (National Democratic Union)

UGB: Unión Guerrera Blanca (Union of White Warriors, paramilitary)

UNO: Unión Nacional Opositora (National Union of Opposition)

UR-19: Universitarios Revolucionarios 19 de Julio (19 July Revolutionary Students)

UTC: Unión de Trabajadores del Campo (Union of Rural Workers).

About This Book

They Won't Take Me Alive (*No Me Agarran Viva*) was created to fulfil a promise to Javier, Eugenia's husband, who wished he were a writer, in order to be able to tell Eugenia's story. Claribel Alegría *is* a writer and, together with the research undertaken by her husband and the testimonies of many of Eugenia's comrades-in-arms, has recounted the development of her political struggle. Not only was this a struggle undertaken against one of the bloodiest and most brutal military régimes within even the aggressively oppressive contexts of many Latin American countries, but it shows the personal struggle of a woman coming to terms with a series of ideological and political steps that lead her to lose her life in a violent confrontation.

But the story is not just Eugenia's. It is that of her suffering and rebellious fellow-nationals, still engaged in waging the 'popular war', against a system that many of them describe here in cruel and personal detail, and for a system that some of them have begun to see realised in the zones liberated by the guerrilla armies of the FMLN. And it is a book dedicated to Salvadorean women engaged in political struggle, to Ana Patricia (Eugenia's daughter), to the next generation and a new civilisation.

They Won't Take Me Alive

One

Eugenia dropped to the ground and undertook her own inspection of the arms cache hidden under the truck, checking that each rifle was thoroughly wrapped in rags to protect it from the dust. She reached out and attempted to rattle one of them. Impossible. They were securely fixed and completely hidden from view.

She stood up again, slapped the dust from her jeans and carefully wiped her hands with a handkerchief. She put it back into her pocket and said in a steady voice: 'It's time, comrades. Let's go.'

Two of the young men climbed into the back of the truck. The third took the driver's seat and Eugenia opened the garage doors.

The truck started up, reversed out into the street, and waited while the young woman closed the garage doors and seated herself beside the driver.

They left behind the comfortable suburb of San Salvador and headed out on the highway to Ilopango airport.

It was 17 January 1981. A week earlier the Farabundo Martíí National Liberation Front (FMLN) had begun its general offensive. The guerrilla forces brought the country to a standstill during the first three days, achieving most of their military objectives in the interior. Several garrisons were immobilised in regional capitals.

The general strike began on 13 January. Most factories surrounding San Salvador were closed down, but the capital itself was a harder nut to crack. The Christian Democrat military junta had concentrated its élite strategic forces there, and the troops had been put on the alert the day before the offensive. The government reacted swiftly, moving in troops to requisition public transport and forcing shops in the city centre to remain open. Government soldiers patrolled the main streets; mobile units savagely attacked any neighbourhood where people tried to erect barricades.

The junta commandeered every means of communication, including foreign correspondents, to put out the story that the strike had failed. Due to the dearth of effective guerrilla action in San Salvador, most of the capital had not come out in open support of the strike.

However, the struggle continued to develop in several country regions: Chalatenango, Morazán, San Vicente and Suchitoto. The last of these was where Commander Eugenia and her three comrades were now going, taking a consignment of arms and munitions vital to the FMLN campaign there.

As they passed by Ilopango airport, Eugenia was straining to find evidence of the previous week's attack on the Salvadorean air-force hangars. A substantial number of planes and helicopters intended to decimate the population of the guerrilla-controlled zones had either been destroyed or severely damaged by explosive charges set by the FMLN.

Even by screwing up her eyes, Eugenia couldn't make out anything. The commander was short-sighted and none too keen on wearing glasses. On more than one occasion she had confused the Tropigas lorries loaded with gas cylinders with military lorries carrying soldiers.

She sighed. Still ten minutes to go to reach San Martín, where the problems would start. She leaned back in her seat, closed her eyes, and her thoughts drifted back to her last meeting with Javier and Ana Patricia.

Ana Patricia couldn't understand farewells. Who could comprehend such matters at the age of thirteen months? She remained very serious, without passing comment, when Eugenia covered her with kisses, smothered her in a last hug, and handed her over to her father.

It was not for the first time. On many occasions during the child's short life Eugenia had left her in the care of one or other 'aunt' within the organisation, while she set off on some urgent mission that would keep her away from home for several days. This time the farewell had been more intense. But it was impossible to keep the infant at her side throughout the strain, the uncertainty, the constant dangers of the offensive.

Eugenia's responsibilities had tripled in the recent weeks of preparation for this new phase of the war. She thought it better for her daughter to remain with Javier although, she thought, 'The kid's so sweet and I'll miss her terribly.'

She opened her eyes and looked outside. She glanced at her wristwatch – a present from Javier on her last birthday – and closed her eyes again in order to relive the farewell.

It was 4 January. Only thirteen days ago. She had barely three and a half hours to spend with Javier. They conversed intently while Ana Patricia played with her rag-doll.

They had reviewed their seven years together, four of them spent in hiding. They remembered the threatened miscarriage and congratulated themselves on the happy outcome, there in person and tugging at Eugenia's hand, insisting that she come and take a look at a caged bird. Was it going to be the last goodbye?

Ahead lay the outline of San Martín, where they had to take the turning to Suchitoto. There was tough fighting going on over there, and Ricardo, who commanded the Felipe Peña Front, was pressing them for these supplies in order to maintain the military confrontation.

Eugenia had joined the High Command of the Felipe Peña Front at the instigation of Ricardo seven weeks previously. Before that she had dedicated herself to political organisation within the Farabundo Martí Popular Liberation Forces – the FPL – but, on the eve of the general offensive, the commander was in desperate need of someone of proven organisational capacity to disentangle complex logistical and supply problems in the critical region of San Salvador, as well as in La Libertad, Cuscatlán and a part of the Cabañas liberated zones.

Without hesitation, Ricardo chose Eugenia to be head of the supply section of the Front's High Command. A week beforehand, at the time the offensive was launched, he also made her responsible for organising the transport of arms and munitions being taken from the capital to wherever they were most needed.

The commander's journey today was to comply with Ricardo's specific request: two days previously she was woken up at two in the morning at her command post to be told to make the journey back to San Salvador to coordinate arms transport to a centre close to Suchitoto.

Eugenia returned to San Salvador. She sent the arms out the same day, but her comrades returned a few hours later with the news that their contact (to whom they were delivering the shipment) hadn't shown up. The following day another attempt was made, with the same result. The three combatants charged with the task were not new to it, but the zone between San Martín and Suchitoto was under army surveillance and infiltrated by armed members of the Democratic Nationalist Organisation (ORDEN) – paramilitary peasant groupings in the pay of the army – and it wasn't easy to establish the reason for the failed rendezvous.

Obviously something was going wrong. Eugenia decided to accompany them on their third journey to ensure that her exact orders were being followed. She wasn't under any specific obligation to accompany this arms consignment but, as Ricardo was to say months later, 'She had thoroughly assimilated her duty as part of the army hierarchy. Fundamental responsibility rests with the commander – the buck stopped with her. She could not offer the excuse that what's-his-name had slipped up.'

The truck took the left-hand fork at San Martín. Eugenia straightened herself, alert. The country's eastern zone was still risky during this, the second week of the offensive. Battles still persisted in Morazán, San Vicente, Zacatecoluca, San Miguel and Suchitoto, where Ricardo's guerrillas were in control of the town's outskirts and continued exerting pressure on the barracks. There was virtually no traffic on the highway.

The truck in which Eugenia and her three comrades were now travelling was the one that had made identical trips on the two preceding days. As this was the third time it was bound to arouse the suspicions of any military detachment. However, there was no alternative: Ricardo needed the arms and the ammunition.

The four travelled 'officially' and unarmed. Their papers

were in order and they had each memorised their cover story on which they relied to get out of a possible mishap. According to the story, they were on their way to Ernesto's uncle's farm to collect hens, eggs and greenstuff, because food was becoming scarce inside the capital.

Minutes became hours as they travelled north along the deserted highway. They left behind them the town of Tecomatepe with the huge volcano to its left, and took the road straight ahead. A jeep containing four soldiers appeared on the other side of the road. It was heading for San Martín.

Without shifting her position, Eugenia raised her voice so that the comrades in the back could hear: 'It's the enemy,' she said. 'Keep calm and keep talking.'

The jeep passed them without slowing down.

'Phew!' exclaimed Mauricio when it had gone out of sight. 'They didn't suspect anything, didn't even spare us a look.'

They continued their journey, and in a few minutes reached the Tenancingo crossroads.

'Here it is,' she said, 'on the right.'

'I know *that*,' Ernesto answered impatiently. 'I know this route by heart.'

'Sorry!' said Eugenia with a smile. 'I was talking to myself.'

They took the dirt road, leaving a column of dust behind them. After five minutes Ernesto braked and turned left into the entrance of a small farm with a sign that read 'Santa Teresita'. He parked the car beneath a flame tree, out of sight of the road.

'We've arrived,' he said. 'Right, Eugenia?'

'Yes,' she replied, looking at her watch, 'and still ten minutes to go. Why don't we get out and see what's happening?'

She sent Luis to guard the entrance, left Ernesto behind the wheel and went into the shack with Mauricio. They lifted up two of the table legs, and then the other two. No message. They returned to the truck and got inside to wait. Ten minutes. Twenty. Nothing.

Eugenia wrote a note: 'We came three times. We'll try the other place on Sunday at the same time.'

She got down from the truck again, folded the scrap of paper and placed it under one of the table legs in the shack.

'Let's hurry, Ernesto,' she said, getting back into the truck. 'This place is hot. We can't wait around any more.'

Ernesto revved up. He waited in the entrance until Luís reappeared between the bushes and clambered back into the truck. Eugenia looked gloomy. She was biting her lower lip.

'Let's hope we have word from Ricardo on our return,' she said. 'The alternative is more dangerous, but at least we can take the other road.'

The four fell silent. Ernesto turned left when they reached the asphalted road, and they drove through the village.

On the way out of Tecomatepe there's a gentle curve to the right and then a sharper one to the left. The saloon car appeared opposite just as Ernesto had straightened up from the second curve. It was going at an even speed.

'Three, in civilian clothes,' Eugenia warned Mauricio and Luís. 'Keep an eye on them.'

The saloon went by and disappeared round the curve.

'The man in the back seat turned to look at us,' said Mauricio in a voice which revealed his tension.

'Hurry, Ernesto,' ordered Eugenia, looking out of the rear window.

'Shit,' muttered Mauricio, as the saloon reappeared. 'They're chasing us.'

'Step on it, Ernesto,' said Eugenia urgently. 'We have to get to the San Francisco crossroads.'

The truck accelerated but the saloon following them was more powerful and gradually closed the distance between them. Eugenia turned round and looked ahead, seeking out the crossroads they needed. It had come into sight. She looked behind again.

'Another!' shouted Ernesto. 'They've trapped us!'

A truck similar to theirs appeared at the intersection. Two men leaped from the back and pointed rifles at them.

'Go up the embankment on your left!' shouted Eugenia. 'They won't take us alive!'

Above the noise of the engine, bursts of sub-machine-gun fire rang out.

Two

Eugenia's real name was Ana María Castillo Rivas. She was born in San Salvador on 7 May 1950. Eugenia was a premature baby and had a twin sister who died during the delivery. She was a delicate child throughout her early years, requiring continual medical attention.

Her parents were Nicaraguan and politically opposed to Somoza.[1] They settled in El Salvador for political reasons a few years before Eugenia was born. They were both devout Catholics and enjoyed a comfortable standard of living. Eugenia's education as a Christian pointed to the direction that her life would later take. Her concern to help the poor and under-privileged took her, little by little, towards a stage where she was ready to join the struggle for her country's liberation.

At the time of Eugenia's birth, El Salvador was ruled by a junta composed of two civilians and three members of the armed forces, all of whom had been instrumental in deposing General Salvador Castañeda Castro eighteen months earlier. Restricted elections followed on 14 September 1950, and Colonel Oscar Osorio assumed presidential office for a six-year term.

The new 1950 constitution, the first since the 1932 massacre,[2] permitted industrial workers to organise and join trade unions. In contrast the peasants, who constituted over

---

[1] The military dictator, whose family had ruled for three generations. He fled into exile with the triumph of the Sandinista revolution in July 1979.
[2] 30,000 civilians, mainly students and peasants, were mown down by the military police.

60 per cent of the population, continued to be barred from organising in the countryside.

Osorio lost no time in exploiting the trade-union clause to create a government-sponsored association, one that could be counted on to give unqualified support to his Party of National Reconciliation. A sudden rise in coffee prices boosted the Salvadorean economy and brought an influx of money into government coffers.

In the wish to justify the title of his '1948 Revolution', Osorio launched a programme for building state schools and subsidised housing, allowing hangers-on and members of his administration to line their pockets at the Treasury's expense. It was his administration that constructed the River Lempa dam, with the aim of supplying the country with sufficient electricity to generate a programme of rapid industrialisation.

Eugenia was scarcely two years old when Osorio's programme of 'social liberalisation' came to an abrupt halt. On 26 September 1952, in the early hours of the morning, the police and security forces seized over a hundred political dissidents, among them trade unionists, students, intellectuals and leaders of the 'New Action' opposition party.

Within hours, Osorio announced that a communist plot to overthrow the government had been uncovered, and declared a state of siege and the suspension of all constitutional rights.

Among those arrested, tortured and imprisoned was Salvador Cayetano Carpio, leader of the Bakers' Union, and his wife Tulita, who was twenty-eight at the time.[1]

Tulita, who came from a humble working-class family, recalled her childhood and her integration into the revolutionary process in the following words:

From a very early age I found myself obliged to go out to work in order to contribute financially to our household. I began work

---

[1] Cayetano Carpio (Commander Marcial) described the tortures they both underwent in his book, *Secuestro y Capucha* (*Kidnap and Hooding* – a reference to prisoners being hooded so they could not identify their torturers and to increase their disorientation).

in little shops, and then transferred to a fizzy drinks and beer factory called 'La Cascada'.

I stayed on there for a number of years and it was there I entered the trade-union movement. I am talking about 1948 when I was twenty-four. At that time it was forbidden to organise trade unions, but an association existed, the Association of Carbonated Drinks Workers.

In 1950, when Colonel Osorio was in power, and when trades-union organisations were authorised, we began to struggle to set one up. It was then I met Commander Marcial. He was on the executive of the Bakers' Union.

Tulita also gave the following account of their arrest and imprisonment:

They picked us up on 26 September 1952. We lived in a shack and at six in the morning the police came and hammered on the door. My mother got up and opened it. They told her, 'We're looking for a thief we know has taken refuge here.'

'There must be some mistake,' she told them. 'No thief has got in here.'

'Leave it out, he's in here all right.'

As they persisted, I got up too, and asked who they were looking for.

'Get dressed,' they ordered.

That's exactly how the police are. They began searching the room and knocking things about, and I began to protest, telling them that what they were doing was outrageous, and asking why they were abusing us like that.

They informed me: 'We don't have to give answers to you. We'll be taking the lot of you in.'

At this Marcial got up and asked me for some water. I went to get some from the sink, and when I handed it to him he threw it into the policeman's face and took to his heels. Other guards stopped behind to keep an eye on me. After a while he was brought back and I saw he was soaked in blood.

'What happened, did they beat you?' I asked him.

'No, it's nothing,' he answered, and they took us off. I was taken along too, they loaded us both into the truck.

There were already about a hundred people detained at the police station when we arrived there. They'd obviously started early on in the day with their detentions. There were workers, intellectuals and a colleague from the bakery called Fidelina Raymundo. They put me into the same cell as her. They put us in the first cell and Marcial into the second. Later on they brought in another woman whose son was a member of the union executive. They were searching for him and, when they couldn't find him, they picked up his mother. They also pulled in another woman with her daughter.

They hooded me for differing lengths of time, but the cruellest torment was having to watch them torturing my husband.

I spent eleven months in prison. We only got out when we were being transferred to a hiding place on the day that the teacher Celestino Castro succeeded in fleeing from the prison. They were taking us into hiding because a search was on for some political criminals. They always did that so our where-abouts should remain secret. The teacher had taken this oppor-tunity to break out, and this created quite a stir. They told us the teacher would be fomenting a scandal outside the jail. The same night they removed eleven o. us political prisoners being held there, and dumped us on the Honduran border. Only four remained behind, as my husband explained in his book.

Once in Honduras we were held at Nacaome for three days. From there we embarked in a sailing boat out of the port of San Lorenzo and were transported to Amapala. They told us that from then on the city would be our prison, and that we should look for work, as there we'd have to remain. They didn't even allow us as far as the quayside. We spent roughly a week there, but the Honduran students mobilised and demanded that the Honduran government set us free on Honduran soil. Instead of complying with that demand, they dumped us on the Guate-malan border.

As at that time Arbenz was in power, there our Calvary was at an end.

We spent a year in Guatemala. At first I found work in a children's nursery, then in a Department of Social Security hospital. My husband remained a prisoner. After the hunger strike, they sent him to a penitentiary. While I was still in Guatemala, Arbenz's government was toppled and all we Salvadorean refugees agreed to seek asylum in the embassies. I sought refuge in the Argentine embassy, but then my husband got out of jail so I went on to Mexico.

During this period, El Salvador's newspapers paid scant attention to the detainees or to Osorio's 'disappeared' political dissidents. On the other hand, the president's civic campaign against crime in San Salvador was enthusiastically hailed as 'a flushing-out of thieves', but it was a campaign which left a toll of hundreds of common criminals assassinated by the police. Their corpses were cast into the River Lempa.

The greatest media catch-phrase of the years 1952–4 was the 'communist threat' supposedly encroaching from neighbouring Guatemala, where Colonel Jacobo Arbenz, supported by popular organisations of workers and peasants, had been trying to institute a series of structural reforms, including an agricultural reform that jeopardised the major incursions of the United Fruit Company's banana plantations. The CIA mounted a propaganda campaign that grew inexorably until, in the spring of 1954, the US stooge Carlos Castillo Armas launched an invasion into Guatemala from Honduran territory, with air support courtesy of Anastasio (Tacho) Somoza's Nicaraguan air-force, and succeeded in bringing down Arbenz's government.

This blow was yet another in the interminable list of those the United States has orchestrated against any reformist initiative within their 'backyard' of Central America and the Caribbean.

Eugenia was, of course, unaware of all these episodes in her country's history. She was barely four years old, and was busy playing with her dolls and struggling to shake off a series of childhood illnesses.

She was the second of seven children and the eldest of three daughters. Her next sister, Marta, was born in 1957, the year in which Eugenia began to attend the Convent School of the Assumption in San Salvador. Her youngest sister, Ondina, was born in 1962. The two younger girls were later to follow Eugenia's example and became active in El Salvador's freedom movement.

Marta remembered:

Eugenia was a tower of strength to my mother in bringing us up. She was mother to the little ones. From the time she was small, she was my parents' right hand in our daily instruction. We all had a deep and affectionate respect for her.

One of the most important things I remember from my childhood is the great sense of duty she had with regard to her responsibilities as the eldest sister. There was never the faintest trace of negligence or any lack of tenderness in her care. She always showed a great affection in her behaviour towards us.

Although there was quite a gap in our ages we weren't aware of it, because she was always outgoing and knew how to place herself on the same level as other people. I always had utter confidence in her.

Our family was of a progressive turn of mind, above all my father. We were educated in that vein and Eugenia, from when she was quite young, was always keen to take part in literacy programmes, not only for humanitarian but for religious reasons.

She always wanted to try and help others. If there was an earthquake, she would be there; if there were literacy classes, catechism day schools, any activity to serve the needs of others, she'd be right in there. She participated in youth groups from about the age of fifteen onwards, and all this activity directed itself towards a permanent yearning to seek out something she could give herself to.

At home we were also brought up to have respect for other people. My father was pretty devout, but his thinking was liberal.

He was a Nicaraguan and against Somoza. He spent quite some time in exile. This gave our education its characteristic stamp of being neither conservative nor reactionary.

We were a very united family. We had a consciousness of brother- and sisterhood, and respect for the authority of our elders. For example, my parents went off to Nicaragua and we youngsters stayed behind, all looking after one another.

My mother was very devout, more religious than my father, and more mystical. While we were helping others, my mother was helping us. She even prided herself on the fact that we didn't become dope-smokers or junkies or turn out crazy. She was proud of our spirit of curiosity. As matters began to take an increasingly political turn, and Eugenia became more deeply involved, her response was to seek to protect us. She wanted to prevent us from becoming even more committed but this was out of her affection for us, not because she held reactionary political views.

Her youngest sister, Ondina, remembered the influence Eugenia exercised during her childhood.

It was Eugenia who gave me my basic instruction. It was the same for Marta, but I was twelve years younger than Eugenia. After our father died, she took me to see our country's slums. I clearly remember her taking me to the Plan Piloto as though to impress upon me the seriousness of the poverty that existed. She always told me how important it was to help children, how much it mattered to play with them, never overlooking the fact that I too was a little girl.

She was a mother to me. When my periods started, she was the one who came and explained how to put on a sanitary towel, she who helped me begin to understand those sorts of things, and all this made me regard her as a mother to me. Whenever chores needed to be done in the home, it was she who told us we had to clean the windows. Not my mum, her.

Dad's personality was like Eugenia's. He was an expansive, outgoing character and a very kindly person. A fine man. We all admired him enormously. He was very highly educated and very demanding. Eugenia had his dynamism, his high level of activity. My mother was a steadier character. Eugenia had the characteristics of both. Physically, she looked more like my father: his straight hair, his eyebrows, his eyes. My mother was fair with light eyes. Eugenia was dark.

'My father played an active part in the Church,' Marta continued. 'He was a Christian leader, a militant. He was the president of a heap of clubs, right up to the Lions. He had real leadership quality. He was in the habit of informing us: "Today we won't attend the local church, we'll hear Mass in the slums, because that way you'll learn how the children there live, and won't waste your food." '

'Once, at our home,' Ondina recalled, 'he put up a sign in the kitchen which read: "10,000 die of hunger every day." Servants took care of the essential chores, we took care of the rest. They brought us up according to their principles within the framework of our bourgeois education.'

María Elena de Girón knew Eugenia 'since I was a little child'. They were both virtually the same age. They grew up on the same street in San Salvador's Colonia Centro América, and went to school at Convent of the Assumption.

María Elena remembered:

Their home was truly Christian. At mealtimes their father always read the Bible aloud. When their father died, Eugenia's mother carried on his close contact with the churches. She was a pretty powerful woman, and ruled the home with a rod of iron.

Eugenia was never a leader at school. She is remembered best for her cheerful personality and because she was an obedient daughter. She was very well-loved, she had a place in the hearts of all her fellows. She never refused her friendship or her assistance to anyone.

When we reached the fourth grade, we enrolled in the Christian Student Youth Movement [JEC], which had highly disciplined methods of working.

The JEC's work was very much inspired by the Church's new pastoral concern. We met weekly, and the meetings followed a basic pattern we laid down. We had to analyse a facet of student life, and assess all its aspects in the light of readings taken from the Bible. What attitude we should assume to such-and-such. The technique was to examine, judge and act. Action then implied concrete undertakings.

Eugenia played a large part in all this. We used to visit the Bloom, the children's hospital. We had lunch at school and then worked as volunteers in the afternoon. They had an operating theatre, a premature babies' unit and a children's clinic. One couldn't but be moved by so much suffering. We minded the children like mothers.

We also went out to take catechism classes in the schools of the Lourdes and Quiñones slums. We experienced the physical hardships borne by the residents, their living conditions, at first hand. We couldn't remain indifferent to their material needs. Campaigns were organised to build houses, to buy building materials, etcetera. We always worked as a team, Eugenia had no use for individualistic acts of heroism.

We joined the JEC in 1967, and continued through until 1969. The work soon assumed extra-curricular dimensions. Both Catholic and lay schools participated. Later, nearly all the JEC leaders moved on into the guerrilla movement. For example, Rafael Arce became an ERP[1] commander. He's dead now.

It is possible to observe a near-linear development throughout Eugenia's adolescence: the obedient daughter

---

[1] Ejército Revolucionario del Pueblo (People's Revolutionary Army).

from a religious family fulfilling her duties alongside her girlfriends, learning working techniques at school and in the JEC. Her world was widening, showing her the poverty and suffering of less-favoured classes. She preferred to work as one of a team rather than to set herself apart. Perhaps due to this youthful discipline she would later encounter doubts over her capacity to lead.

The two friends parted in 1969. María Elena went to study in the United States, and Eugenia went on a missionary project to Guatemala. It was the first time she had left her family.

María Elena continued:

It had a big effect on Eugenia, she became more independent there, she developed as a person. She worked as a children's teacher, and did a bit of every sort of community work.

Perhaps the most important thing in all those years occurred when she finished her studies. She was involved in missionary activities. The school boasted an Association of Missionaries of the Assumption formed by the most devout girls, those with a willingness to help others. They spent a year working in the villages or in urban areas.

Eugenia went to Guatemala in 1969 and worked among the Indians, always harbouring political worries but without any outlet for them. What most preoccupied her was the astonishing poverty and exploitation, which she discovered had a political rationale exceeding its merely religious explanation.

In January 1969, Eugenia went with a small group of missionaries to Cabricán, a little village in the Quetzaltenango region of Guatemala. She spent a year working there among the poorest peasants of the highlands; a year that prepared and strengthened her for the work in which she would immerse herself for several years.

Eugenia's husband Javier (although they hadn't as yet met), was able to re-create an account of that period from the conversations he had with her:

Her sense of injustice was accentuated by the poverty she encountered in Cabricán, above all in relation to the racism she came across regarding the Indians. On the one hand, this sensitivity was the over-riding factor, and on the other there was her growing need to get at the root of the problem. The question was framing itself: how come our people live under a system of such injustice? Why do our people suffer so much exploitation? She began to consider the inherent contradiction between rich and poor, between the exploiters and exploited, between the oppressors and oppressed. She began to come to terms with the fact that only the people themselves can resolve that problem.

She reevaluated her experience in Cabricán in order to see more clearly where the roots of the problem lay, and to formulate appropriate questions without being able as yet to find all the answers, without coming up with a specifically political response. It was then she realised that it was the people who had to provide the answer. The part she had to play was in helping these people, being a part of the process.

It was during Eugenia's stay in Guatemala that the 'football war' between El Salvador and Honduras erupted. That event, which appeared tragi-comic when seen from the outside, had causes – however far-fetched they seemed – profoundly based in the economies of both countries.

The 'modernisation' process initiated by Osorio and continued by his successor, Colonel José María Lemus, collapsed due to the fact that the landowning oligarchy paid starvation wages in the countryside in order to secure their profits, while the industrial and technological innovations of President Kennedy's 'Alliance for Progress' tried to encourage a higher level of income and living standards among the masses, in order to create a national consumer market to absorb the new products.

The conflict was won by the oligarchy: country workers' wages remained stagnant and the native and international technologists had to invent the Central American Common Market (the MCCA) in order to create an outlet for the abundant industrial products of El Salvador and Guatemala.

In its turn, the MCCA came up against the uneven industrial development of the five Central American countries. Honduras, Nicaragua and Costa Rica had fallen behind their neighbours to the north, and soon found themselves flooded with cheap products (entering from Guatemala and El Salvador) which got in the way of any normal development of national industries in these three countries. It seemed as if they were destined to become sub-dependencies of the already dependent and trans-nationalised economies of El Salvador and Guatemala.

Honduras saw itself as particularly damaged by El Salvador's industrial competence. President López Arellano was pressured into launching a campaign against Salvadorean products by the bourgeois lobby within his country. There was a further serious imbalance between the two countries: the demographic one. While at that time El Salvador had a density of 158 inhabitants per square mile, Honduras had a scant 23.

Since the crushing of the 1932 uprising, every year thousands of Salvadorean peasants filtered over the border, settling in tiny subsistence farms. For reasons of historical necessity, Salvadoreans are very hard-working and the emigrants prospered. In this way, by 1969 the number of Salvadorean emigrants inside Honduras topped 300,000.

The Honduran government, under pressure from the oligarchy, the local bourgeoisie and the forces of imperialism, decided in May 1969 to institute an agrarian reform dispossessing the Salvadoreans of the 'illegal' lands, and giving them instead to Honduran peasants who were themselves landless.

Honduras became the cradle of an anti-Salvadorean campaign that was met with reciprocal anger in El Salvador, culminating in two bloody football matches between teams representing each country, which degenerated into national-chauvinist confrontations.

A few days later the Salvadorean army invaded Honduran territory. After four days of struggle costing some 4,000 lives, the Organisation of American States achieved a ceasefire between the two countries and a precarious truce that would last for twelve years.

The Central American Common Market was shattered, leading to a general crisis within Salvadorean industry. The growing level of unemployment in El Salvador was made visibly worse by the return of thousands of Salvadorean peasants who had been expropriated from their Honduran landholdings.

Eugenia returned from her mission in Guatemala at the start of 1970 and enrolled in the José Simeón Cañas Catholic University. Bureaucratic problems within the university frustrated her intention of following a sociology course. She took up a second option and began to study social psychology.

'In reality it's unclear whether her course was in fact a social psychology one,' said Javier. 'It was more like general psychology, plain and simple, which never met what she was really seeking. At the same time, Eugenia continued to make academic progress and advanced as a student.'

In addition to attending lectures, Eugenia enrolled in University Catholic Action (ACUS) and again took up social work in the poor districts of San Salvador.

In the middle of 1970 Eugenia's father hurried to the rescue of a drowning child swimming in the treacherous Pacific Ocean. He succeeded in saving the boy, carried him in his arms on to the beach and collapsed on the sand, dead.

'He caught hold of the boy,' Ondina told me. 'He carried him out of the surf and had to hold him over his own head. Either his death was due to the effort, or to a seizure, or perhaps he suffered a heart attack. Most likely it gave him a heart attack. He had a problem with his heart.'

'My father dying in that way, through saving a boy's life, made its mark on us,' Marta said. 'My dad would have done as much for anyone.'

The family tragedy changed Eugenia's plans. By day, she helped her mother in the business her father had left to them, and attended evening lectures at the university. In addition to this heavy workload she continued with University Catholic Action (ACUS) but, as had happened before with the JEC, she found social work unsatisfying.

Javier went on:

ACUS' work in the poorer districts also failed to provide her with the answer she was searching for. She didn't find this to be the way for her to make a more decisive contribution to solving the problems of poverty.

At university she began to obtain access to a lot of books and this helped her gain in understanding. She began to worry herself about arriving at a more scientific comprehension of the problem. She began to get to know how capitalism works, the issue of class struggle, not only in terms of rich and poor but of capitalist exploitation, and that our countries are dependencies of North American imperialism. This was going on throughout her university career. Our comrade took a decisive step forward. She abandoned ACUS and joined a movement called the University Socialist Movement, run by the social-democratic tendency National Revolutionary Party and now part of the Revolutionary Democratic Front (FDR).

Eugenia continued working at all three things, but became increasingly interested in politics.

Marta added:

My mother has a very strong character, and Eugenia inherited this from her. My mother never became overwhelmed in the face of difficulties. There is an inherent contradiction in this. People would say to us: 'Your mother is a widow and you have to help her out', but the truth of the matter is that she would never be helped. She ran the business all on her own. Previously, during the daytime, Eugenia used to help her, and at night she completed the chores and studied. Later on she abandoned the income-producing work and carried on with the housework and attending university.

I spent several months with my mum but from then on we were committed to the revolutionary struggle. Ondina was still at school. I left home, I really wasn't able to help mum out. She was capable of maintaining the business, and we had skills more relevant to the people.

For several years there had been an internal disagreement within the Salvadorean Communist Party (PCS) over whether to continue their 'legal and electoral' line or whether they should adopt a more aggressive position, a politico-military strategy.

The crisis came to a head in 1970 and Salvador Cayetano Carpio (Commander Marcial) resigned his position as secretary-general of the Salvadorean Communist Party and left the organisation. He vanished from the scene along with a handful of sympathisers and his clandestine existence commenced. On 19 April the FPL was set up as a politico-military organisation postulating a new strategy for the Salvadorean people's struggle: a prolonged popular war.

A number of sound reasons exist for doubting the possibilities of a guerrilla war in El Salvador. The country's small size, its dense population and lack of terrain suited to guerrilla operations made one assume that the enterprise would end in disaster. In addition the failure of the *foquista*[1] enterprises at the end of the 1960s in Guatemala, Nicaragua, Peru and Bolivia, had generated a wave of pessimism and doubt as to whether guerrilla tactics were viable in the face of sophisticated counter-insurgency measures the United States was offering to the Latin American armies.

Cayetano Carpio's clandestine group didn't bother to think up a name for themselves during their first year in existence. In an interview given in February 1980, when his identity was made public for the first time, Marcial said:

> That was an easy decision, taken at the organisation's earliest meeting, and for a number of reasons under consideration at the time. It was grounded in the necessity of training ourselves within a new discipline as revolutionaries, within a revolutionary context established on the basis of sacrifices that would be demanded of us by the path we were taking: the way of prolonged war, a way that hadn't been tried in our country.
>
> So it became essential to uncover our capacity for advancing along this path, and whether we as individuals were capable of transforming ourselves in order to follow it – if we were able to acquire the necessary political context, realise the necessary sacrifices, renounce normal life and exchange it for secrecy and the total compartmentalisation of one's existence.
>
> In other words, it spelt out the necessity of immolating oneself in the crucible of practice, one could affirm it as a test, and see if we were capable of translating theory into practice. And this only life itself could tell us.

Those traditionalists remaining within the PCS began to enter into a pact with the Christian Democratic Party (PDC)

---

[1] Guerrilla bases in remote parts of the countryside which set out to convert the most exploited sectors of the population.

and the National Revolutionary Movement (MNR), a small social-democratic party. The communists adopted the name National Democratic Union (UDN) for themselves, and the coalition of the three parties became known as the National Union of Opposition (UNO).

José Napoleón Duarte was UNO's presidential candidate in the 1972 elections and obtained, without doubt, the majority of votes, but as usual the Party of National Conciliation (PCN) won on the recounts and Colonel Arturo Armando Molina assumed the presidency in July 1972.

That year's electoral fraud clearly demonstrated that the door to political change, by means of democratic elections, had been closed by the military and the oligarchy. The experience was to be repeated with yet more scandalous frauds in the 1974 and 1977 elections.

It was obvious by 1972 that Marcial and his companions had chosen the only path leading to the prospect of change: the way of armed struggle and prolonged popular war.

When Eugenia left Catholic Action to affiliate to the University Socialist Movement, she took a decisive step forward. She plainly understood that the disastrous social and economic conditions inside El Salvador demanded a political and not a charitable solution. The movement, however, did not offer the dynamic way through she was looking for and, as previously occurred with the Catholic organisations, she didn't succeed in slaking her thirst for more positive action.

Back at home, the disagreements were multiplying. Eugenia's mother and her older brothers did not approve of her left-wing political activities.

Marta said nostalgically:

Our home used to be fairly united, but in time the war divided us. The war led some of us to take up revolutionary positions, others to advance class interests, and pulled us apart as a family.

There was conflict with my brothers. I don't know why, it seemed to run in their blood. One brother, the youngest, was fine. Eugenia's influence over him proved decisive. She was always very emotional and the clashes with our mum shocked her a good deal. She identified a lot with my mum. She tested herself against her. Family pressure was considerable, especially for my eldest brother. Eugenia argued a lot with Mum, there was a period when it was a daily occurrence. My mother was a very considerate person, but she isn't a Marxist and never will be.

Colonel Molina's fraudulent assumption of presidential power had a brief sequel some weeks later, when the army's constituent section – a group of young officers in charge of San Salvador's principal regiments – rose in protest. While such forces of repression as the National Guard, the National Police and the Customs Officers confronted the rebels, the Defence Minister Humberto Romero picked up a phone and called the headquarters of CONDECA (the Central American Defence Council) in Quarry Heights, in the Panama Canal Zone. Within hours, the sky over San Salvador was speckled with the military aeroplanes of the Nicaraguan and Guatemalan air-forces. They bombarded the rebel barracks and, eighteen hours later, the military rebellion was crushed, taking a toll of 200 corpses.

Colonel Molina unleashed a wave of repression against his opponents, torturing and assassinating their leaders or, in most instances, expelling them from the country.

The military uprising in 1972 taught the Salvadorean people another lesson: it was impossible to alter the political situation within the country either by electoral methods or by means of a military coup. CONDECA, orchestrated by the United States, would never allow for any change within the Central American status quo.

It was through the University Socialist Movement, in the search for a deeper connection with her people, that Eugenia met her future husband, Javier. He reconstructed her political education:

> She continued reading, she continued asking questions, and in 1974 (I always remember this) she arrived at her conclusion: the need to align herself directly with the workers. With an embryonic self-education in Marxism, she concluded that it was the Salvadorean workers who had to respond, that it was the workers and peasants who had to resolve their own problems, and in order for this to happen what emerged as the fundamental issue was the struggle for power.

Eugenia underwent a gradual development at university, thanks to the books she picked her way through, and the experience she gained from her close involvement with the people. She had to ally herself directly with the working class of our country, and began to look for links with the farm labourers. One has to bear in mind that El Salvador is an agricultural country, that the farm labourer and peasant have a very important part to play. This weighed heavily with her at that time; the conditions in the countryside were horrific. She decided to form closer ties there and that decision led to the path on which we met.

Without going into my own recent past, this decision of hers coincided with my arrival at similar conclusions at the start of 1974, even though via a different process. At that time, knowing of the struggle in which our people were engaged, I was certain that it was necessary for our Salvadorean people to enter further into the revolutionary struggle. I had also reached the conclusion that the only way forward for our people was by force of arms. To me, that was as clear as daylight, although I was yet to join a particular organisation. At this time, my first concern was to ally myself directly with the workers. That was how I came to pledge myself to the revolutionary work taking place in the countryside, alongside the Christian Federation of Salvadorean Peasants, an organisation with a Christian Democratic bias and doing a lot of grassroots work in those days.

What interested me was establishing a relationship with people in the countryside, I wanted to make contact with the agricultural working class, and from there to begin to contribute to the workers' revolutionary struggle.

We shared our worries about all this one evening when, as a group of students, we met with some comrades from the Salvadorean University Movement. I joined via the Independent University Students organisation.

We had a discussion about the work to be done in the countryside, and I mentioned that I was in contact with certain leaders and that they were making us a definite proposal of work in the rural areas. In the process of discussion, two of Eugenia's comments aroused my curiosity. One was when she voiced her reasons for wanting to link herself directly with the working classes. She set her desire in the context of wishing to discover, really to get to grips with, what the daily life of the people consisted in, without preconceptions.

Her other remark amounted to a critique of the university

students who 'yearned to' collaborate with the people, who 'yearned to' do all sorts of things, who talked a lot and did nothing.

This took place at the very beginning of April 1974. At the end of the meeting we stayed behind chatting, she introduced herself to us and we agreed a time to lunch together the following day. There was a series of coincidences in the type of questions we were posing. They commanded the attention of each of us.

As a result of that meal we began working together, work that only came to an end with the death of my comrade.

'In 1974 Eugenia was already assuming a political stance,' Ondina recalled. 'She started not returning home, or returning late, missing out on her family responsibilities. There was a change. She no longer obeyed Mum, but only those principles she'd begun to believe in, the organisation's own discipline, etc. In the end, she left home.'

Marta confirmed:

Like Ondina said, Eugenia left home. She went to live in the poor quarter of a small village. She had no money or anything, she only took a blanket with her. I brought food to her. She stayed there for some months until, for security reasons, she was told she had to leave.

She went to live in a small flat. They gave her some kitchen utensils. Mum didn't visit her. When they met up later on, there were always arguments.

As well as continuing with her university studies, Eugenia taught in order to support herself. On leaving home, she redoubled her efforts on behalf of the peasants.

Javier continued:

We gave ourselves to the work in the countryside. We involved ourselves in grassroots organisations. We initiated projects in the same districts, visited the same areas, set up contacts among the same workers and became very affected by the revolutionary choice we were making at that time.

Despite the fact our relationship was so recently formed, the two of us saw ourselves all of a sudden – and particularly after our first meeting with the agricultural workers – as having taken a permanent revolutionary option. We regarded it as our initiation into El Salvador's armed struggle, a choice that there was no way of denying. We were aware that during that period there existed revolutionary politico-military organisations in the countryside.

It seemed clear to me that the only way through was by force of arms. Eugenia hadn't given too much consideration to the problem of violence. However, after two or three conversations she was completely convinced that this was the way forward.

We got together a group of students engaged in agricultural work. We tried to formulate our ideas into a system and to deepen our understanding of Marxism. We slowly developed this way of working, and later consolidated it into the formation of a revolutionary movement, a then tiny revolutionary cell, one cast in the same mould as the war our people had undertaken since 1970, and which sought to contribute to the development of the popular movement, the development of the worker–peasant movement.

Although our immediate tasks lay in the countryside, we organised what later came to be called 'The Movement', which was converted into a quasi-underground movement. Eugenia and I were among the founders of this organisation. From there we began to question ourselves over the nature of the problems of a revolutionary vanguard, and over the political development of the masses. Bit by bit we came to know the other revolutionary organisations then establishing themselves in El Salvador and so our work in the countryside deepened and expanded.

That's how, throughout 1974, we took a committed part in the first stoppages, the first strikes, the first street demonstrations, and the entire process of struggle.

Commander Ricardo worked closely with Eugenia during her time as a peasant organiser, until she went underground. He said:

We were beginning our rapprochement with the agricultural workers primarily in the Aguilares and Guazapa regions. Rutilio Grande was the parish priest of Aguilares and El Paisnal, until he was assassinated in 1977.

Eugenia was very clear right from the start. From the first moment she began to work in the countryside she started to encounter problems and difficulties at home, as women from her class background do, but this was never allowed to become an obstacle to the development of her work.

I remember that to begin with, given all the problems at home, and all the demands of university and the rest, the issue became one of whether she could actually cope with the job. She had to keep making excuses to others as a way of keeping up with her agricultural work. She did not simply work among the peasants and casual labourers but also shared their daily lives. It wasn't a matter of undertaking a project in a spirit of paternalism, as a religious sacrifice, to help these people get on their feet, but rather one of submerging herself in their lives, in order to rise with them in pursuit of a new alternative.

Eugenia underwent a process of proletarianisation, though hardly a romantic one. Her level of work in the countryside was formidable. From the very first she was an outstanding organiser. She showed all the signs of knowing how to integrate herself into her field of work, sharing the same lifestyle as her peasant comrades, without giving rise to conflict; knowing how to carry the essence of revolutionary morality forward without letting the fact that she was among so many men cause any kind of problem.

Furthermore, this signalled something very important, not only in her life, but in terms of our revolutionary work and a growth of political consciousness among our working-class comrades.

Eugenia started work in the Guazapa region. After her death I ran across a number of comrades who began to ask after her. Everyone in her area remembers her with deep affection and admiration. To a great extent, it is to her they owe their initiation into the entire revolutionary process.

I think she'd already left home. She had a tiny room of her own. I used to go and visit her in this little room and we would sit around there, chatting together. Then we would go on to Pop's for an ice-cream, in order to settle any outstanding questions.

Here and now, what's important to underline is that this friend of ours, in addition to her agriculturally based work, was participating in structures that incorporated a grander political vision, structures that presupposed a certain level of discipline and vigour as far as her militancy was concerned.

Two important factors are relevant here. The first was her post as an organiser and her ability to direct events. A directive ability that indubitably obliged her to assume the fullest possible responsibility. A commitment that went hand-in-hand to match her ability. At first this induced a degree of fear in her. Not fear of giving herself completely but, as she would say, of not being able to take things step by step. So she overcame her reservations, and took the leap.

The second factor was her enormous capacity for work. Not only for working on a specific task, but also for relating it to the surrounding issues, all of which were directed towards the same goal. It was within that process that one could observe her tremendous spirit of comradeship. Eugenia was instrumental in bringing many comrades into the revolutionary process. She helped them to take the decisive step.

Her entire involvement within the organisation was characterised by a mood of happiness. As she became more and more involved, she seemed to become increasingly happy, and she passed this on. Around this time she was firm friends with my girlfriend, who found herself in a similar situation. This was the period of growth and transition towards a more definite and radical position. From the first moment onwards, Eugenia could clearly perceive the need for her work to lead into the development of the armed struggle.

'Towards the end of 1974,' Javier said, 'we became convinced that no other alternative existed. Our experience was that the most elementary demands of the peasants would always be met by the military dictatorship's usual response of repression and bloodshed. We lived through a lot of that in 1974. Each legally acceptable channel was only another weapon in the oppressors' hands, reinforcing our theory that the people had no other option but the armed struggle: revolutionary violence was the only possible means to achieving liberation. This conviction ran deep in the two of us by the end of 1974.'

It was under Molina's rule that the Salvadorean government began to employ 'modern' forms of repression against resistance from the popular forces. Three weeks after assuming presidential office, in July 1972, Molina ordered the troops to occupy the university. He dissolved the governing council and expelled the rector from the country, along with the deans and the principal university administrators. The university remained closed for two years.

On Molina's express authority, Colonel José (Chele) Medrano created ORDEN (the Democratic Nationalist Organisation), a paramilitary organisation based in the city outskirts, but dedicated to sowing terror in the countryside. At the end of 1974 it produced its first 'search and destroy' operation at the massacre of Chinamequita and student unrest started up again.

The students took up cudgels on behalf of the oppressed peasants because at that time the peasants were hardly in a position to rise up in protest themselves. In a country where the only party-political opposition came from an enfeebled Communist Party (that had been virtually leaderless since the 1932 uprising and subsequent defections) and the nascent and timid Christian Democrats, there was not yet a rural guerrilla movement. In fact, to begin with, ORDEN attracted many of its 100,000 members from a peasantry who desperately wanted arms to secure the poor plot of land they actually owned, and the exemption from paying land-tax that membership automatically bestowed. But, most importantly of all, all ORDEN members were issued with identity cards, and without them the rural poor – landless and petty landowners alike – were always open to suspicion of subversive activity.

The US involvement was there from the beginning, in ideology and in practice. ORDEN's *raison d'être* was 'to root out communists' and during the 1970s conservative heyday, members were gathered from the peasantry by tried and tested carrot-and-stick techniques. On the one hand, membership guaranteed weapons to defend a margin of land, however meagre; on the other, ORDEN identity cards protected the possessors from constant harassment.

Those casting suspicion and, all too often, administering rough justice, were the ORDEN members themselves. As in any witch-hunt, personal points were doubtless made, scores settled, and land or remuneration acquired simply by the association of a particular name with an ill-defined 'subversive activity'. In 1970 El Salvador's General Staff's College Review published an article on *Communist Subversion and Guerrilla Action*. This defined how, in General Guzmán Aguilar's words, 'it will be necessary for agencies to penetrate governmental dependencies and recruit agents for intelligence networks at the level of villages'. This mutual spying and suspicion became systematised into legalised terror and sadism supervised by the likes of Major Roberto d'Abuisson who, in the 1970s, became the United States' presidential protégé for El Salvador.

The United States input had a decidedly McCarthyite flavour from the start. As early as 1964, the US military was running a Central American Security Communications Network inside each country in the region, operating out of native intelligence services 'to permit police and security agencies . . . to directly communicate information on the identity, movements, activities and plans of subversives and criminals'. The programme was geared to 'rooting out communists' within each Central American country – a task which, in El Salvador in the 1970s, apparently necessitated one Salvadorean in every fifty spying on the other forty-nine.

General Medrano himself believed he was relinquishing more formal links with the National Guard in order to put his capacities at the service of ORDEN – 'to fight the plans and actions of international communism', with the backing of the CIA and the US State Department. The first US military trainers came with a Colonel Arthur Simons of the Green Berets and, again according to Medrano, 'We talked about how we had to indoctrinate the people, because he who had the population wins the war . . . it was almost like a religion'.

It was this US-inspired 'hearts and minds' campaign that the various student organisations Eugenia had worked with were combating, but the scale of ORDEN's atrocities was in itself leading many peasants to seek out the way of armed struggle in self-defence. After their massacre at China-mequita, the sense of outrage was such that the time seemed ripe to build a military initiative.

Javier continued:

At the beginning of 1975, the two of us joined the Farabundo Martí Popular Liberation Forces – the politico-military organisation that Marcial and his comrades had founded five years earlier.

By 1975 Eugenia was completely absorbed in our work. Little by little, she abandoned her university studies. She left the psychology faculty, her thesis still pending. During 1975 she developed her rurally based work substantially, making a major contribution to the Federation of Agricultural Workers. A United Popular Action Front (FAPU) had been founded in mid-1974 as a coalition to protest at the high cost of living. At that time, Eugenia and I were working with the Christian Federation of Salvadorean Peasants (FECCAS), which had no clear political line.

FECCAS had come to be identified with those socially-conscious Christians who had set it up, it was still an organisation finding its way, it had come through a major crisis. It possessed one or two significant leaders of great vision: one of them was Apolinario Serrano (Polín). When FAPU was formed, many organisations banded together, but a number of problems arose around the concept of what a mass coalition ought to be about, and those organisations which were about to form themselves into the Popular Revolutionary Bloc pulled out, leaving only FAPU alongside FECCAS, the strongest organisations.

The demonstrations mounted by FAPU in 1974 and through until FECCAS' withdrawal in June 1975 were effectively made up of FECCAS supporters and other student organisations, including a very small group of the teachers' section.

FECCAS' withdrawal was precipitated by an ideological crisis about what a rural revolutionary organisation ought to be, and over the rôle of a popular front. This rift marred the whole process of ideological struggle taking place at that time between the Salvadorean revolutionary organisations that today find themselves in the FMLN-FDR. FECCAS wrote its letter of resignation in June 1975. It had still not been processed by the executive council when the Cathedral was occupied, that July.

FECCAS played a prominent part in the siege, alongside the other groups in the Bloc. It backed the strategy of prolonged popular war put forward by the Popular Liberation Forces (FPL), believing that the peasants' revolutionary struggle would develop within this framework, alongside that of the whole people, and that the joint formation of a mass front would have to be cast within this strategic mould.

The other organisations then making up FAPU disagreed. This was the ultimate cause of the split.

At the end of 1974 and the beginning of 1975, the formation of sectional organisations took place together with their accelerated development. This was above all true of the rural organisations, but students, shanty-town dwellers and others were also involved. It gave another hike to the boom within the mass movement. It fitted our theory of combat, as we called it, whose theme was that the popular masses' struggle for urgent and fundamental rights would cause them to discover fresh methods of struggle that could permit them to advance against a régime whose only replies were bullets and massacres.

In one sense there was a leap forward. Evidence of the boom, which was a giant one, could be noted throughout the country. There was a student demonstration, a rag-day procession that marched through the streets of Santa Ana, and which was put down by means of violence. The students, and above all a group called the 19 July Revolutionary Students (UR-19), planned a demonstration to denounce and condemn the massacre that took place.

The procession left from San Salvador university and went along 25th Street/North Avenue, as though towards Rosales Hospital and Cuzcatlán Park. Up by the Social Security building, where there's the underpass, the army had set up a military operation to cover a vast area, machine-guns and all. They ambushed the demonstration, just as though they were out to ambush an enemy army rather than a peaceful student demonstration. That was where the massacre took place.

This was on 30 July. It has never proved possible to verify the exact number of the dead. Figures rise from perhaps 30 or 40 to 200 deaths. We estimate there must have been near enough 60 killed, with many more wounded and 'disappeared'.

It was during this mobilisation that a comrade who was also a great leader was cut down. His name was Carlos Fonseca. He was leader of the UR-19 student movement and a member of the FPL. He died with the microphone in his hand, while calling on everyone to retreat in order to prevent more comrades being hit by the bullets.

This massacre occurred at a moment when the revolutionary movement was in upsurge. It was the first time in many years that it showed its capacity for responding in such a spirit of defiance.

That same night, on 30 July, a group of Christians called a meeting together with some workers. At that meeting, they took a decision to repudiate and actively respond to the massacre. They decided to seize the Cathedral, to convert it into a public forum for the people and the world.

The occupation of the Cathedral was timed to take place after our comrades' burial. There was a funeral Mass, after which the coffins were carried out to the cemetery, accompanied by the people. Those responsible for the occupation stayed inside.

A series of demands was attached to the denunciation: 'disappeared' colleagues were to be 're-appeared'; responsibility for the massacre should be assigned; and the guilty should be brought to justice.

The funeral Mass provided an enormous concentration of popular groups, attracting the public support of all the grass-roots organisations and their leaders. Those under the FPL's command formed a strong presence.

At this stage there was no Broad Front nor anything of the kind in existence. With the Cathedral as the centre of agitation and accusations, a tributary movement began to flow through-out El Salvador generating a crucial spirit of unification. The popular mobilisation led to an amalgamation that itself bred the formation of the Popular Revolutionary Bloc (BPR). It was a long-awaited resolution, in the sense that it determined how to weld all the mass organisations into a mass revolutionary front, struggling for the rights of each and everyone.

Amid the hubbub surrounding the development of this popular coalition, the Bloc was born as a popular front that led the occupation of the Cathedral. I was the link between the comrades who brought the occupation to its climax and the outside leadership, between the nascent organisation of the BPR and the FPL.

Eugenia remained outside. Her brief was to collaborate with me over questions of security. She was responsible for getting me across between the two sides, as I had to keep going in and out of the Cathedral. She was a part of all that was happening and at the same time occupied in helping in the countryside. She participated in the Bloc's formation in consequence of her work with the peasants, and was a guiding force in the Rural Workers' Federation (FTC) which, as I've already said, is a union of FECCAS and the UTC.

She played an outstanding part in the creation of this union: she took part in the earliest leadership courses, in the first discussions about setting it up, in the elaboration of what would become the initial platform in creating this federation, res-ponsible for amalgamating the two revolutionary rural organ-isations which have since then had a real significance within El Salvador.

Eugenia was gifted with a breadth of understanding that made her a major force in proposing the formation of a mass front. In all her educational work and political formation she succeeded in transmitting, instilling and advancing her case that agricultural workers should link themselves to every grassroots sector, and to the middle class.

Our organisation regards her as a revolutionary pioneer, as a comrade who contributed in a high degree to finding out the forms and formulae for directing the revolutionary struggle of the masses.

During 1975 and 1976 she remained entirely immersed in this grassroots work. She was always to be found in the provinces, sowing the seeds of evolution. She covered a wide number of districts and many tiny villages. Hers was a highly hush-hush enterprise, one that demanded a lot of patience, yet at the same time she was visibly active and combative during our mobilisations.

There wasn't a single mass demonstration in which she didn't participate. She worked alongside great leaders, some of whom are now dead, and they provided the best possible revolutionary education. So it was in the case of Comrade Apolinario Serrano, the famous Polín, who was honoured by our organisation as a member of Central Command and also of its political committee, only two months' before his death in action. Polín stood out as among the greatest popular leaders in El Salvador.

Eugenia received her training alongside leaders such as Justo Mejía, Apolinario Serrano, Felix García. She was partly the teacher and greatly the student of these comrades. Apolinario and Felix always remembered her as a comrade who sowed the revolutionary seed in them and who contributed to their political development. She remembered Polín, Justo Mejía and Felix García as comrades who instilled the true principles of working-class life in her. Together with them, Eugenia initiated and deepened a process of proletarianisation that would, in time, become one of her most notable characteristics.

Eugenia was fully committed to the struggle of the masses throughout these years. However, 1975 and 1976 were two years in which the rumblings of grassroots and armed struggle brought the war in our country to some sort of climax. The repression was intensified, as was the genocide, and the situation become increasingly difficult for both of us, as for every well-known militant.

It was thus, at the end of 1976, the organisation decided that we should go into hiding. This happened at the same time as we were about to be married.

Three

Commander Isabel was one of the people closest to Eugenia when she first began her life as an FPL militant.

It was Isabel who brought her into the organisation and assumed responsibility for her for close on two years, at a time when revolutionary activities were experiencing headlong growth in the whole of the country.

Isabel lived in hiding with Eugenia and Javier, witnessing and participating in some key moments of her revolutionary career. She told me:

I knew Eugenia when she was still a girl joining in the Catholic schools' Christian movements.

She was a gentle and pleasant person, but strong in the convictions she expressed. She had a very attractive personality. Sometimes she gave the impression of being timid and nervous. She didn't talk a lot, but when she did, it was in an impressive manner.

I saw her again on our demonstrations which took place following her return from Guatemala, and we chatted together. She had already acquired a more political train of thought. She was working with peasant organisations, co-ops, doing church-organised Christian social work and courses for our comrades; teaching women how to bath their babies, how to feed them, how to make do with the insubstantial diet they had.

We women comrades were between 16 and 20 years old. We were full of feeling, but we also possessed theories, ideas and propositions that were acquiring maturity through being tested in practice. We were filled with energy and emotions. All that poverty hit us hard.

Eugenia took it all in. She was like one of those sensitive plants that absorb all there is in the atmosphere, but she didn't easily show her emotions; rather she assimilated them.

After this I enlisted for politico-military duties and lost sight of her for a long time. In 1976 Eva, the woman responsible for me, told me only three days before her own death: 'Look, go and fetch Comrade Eugenia.' I didn't know who she meant, so she explained: 'She'll have an orange and be hanging about in Cuzcatlán Park. You'll take a biro up to her,' and she gave me the signal. 'This comrade is about to start her militant activity in the organisation and you'll be responsible for her.'

So I was to enrol her in the FPL. Eva explained our comrade's past record, her notable qualities, her weaknesses, the tasks we would be working on. We were then already in the section involved with the peasant labourers. Eva met her death around that time. Her real name was Elizabeth Ramírez and she was killed at Santa Tecla.

Javier had recruited Eugenia for the organisation. The system is to recruit the comrade, and then transfer her over to whoever is going to be put in charge of her.

Javier and I were in the same collective at the time of Eva's death. Eva was responsible for the two of us and was second-in-command of the collective. We rapidly got together with Javier and began to go over all the things that had been left hanging, in order to work them out. Eva burnt all the records before she died.

I told Javier that I had to make contact with a comrade and was off to meet her.

'Oh,' Javier replied, 'and what's she called?'

'Eugenia.'

'I thought she'd been collected,' he said. 'I thought it was Eva going to meet her.'

Comrade Eva was very brilliant and very careful. No one had revealed Eugenia's identity, so I asked Javier and he told me her name. Then I remember telling myself: 'Hell, I know this one.' She was unaware I was going to fetch her and as Javier still wasn't in the picture, I couldn't tell him.

I went to the meeting. I set off on my walk. I saw her from a long way off, with her orange, her books, her jeans, her Guatemalan shirt and her sandals, her long hair and her glasses. There in front of the chemist in the Cuzcatlán building. It seemed funny that she hadn't noticed me. She was watching everyone that passed, but as I was also in disguise she hadn't recognised me.

I continued walking, walking. I reached her and she spun round to look. I secretly gave her the signal, for no one ever gives it overtly. She turned round to look at me while appearing to cast her eyes over all the people in that park. She glanced at me as though in passing and hey! turned her head and stared at me with a tinge of magic in her look. She started walking towards me and she gave me a big smile and I showed her the signal. We didn't even mention the password but gave one another a huge hug.

When Eugenia saw me approach, she said she'd been in no doubt that I'd come to collect her, but she still stayed still, staring at me and watching my approach, tossing the orange up and down and hop! I pulled out the biro and showed it to her.

So we began to walk and chat and then I told her we were going to work together, and that we'd continue seeing one another. 'First you have to have a programme of studies,' I told her. Eugenia was so excited, so excited.

'Yes, yes,' she said. 'That's great. Magnificent. What a thrill. What a thrill!'

She was in the non-clandestine mass movement, and explained the commitments she'd made to me. There was an assembly, demonstrations. She had to help organise all that. I told her not to worry, and we left the rest for our next meeting.

Ever since 1974 Eugenia had been working to build FECCAS. I was put in charge of her in 1976, '77 and until the middle of 1978. We had the luck, the honour, of proposing her as a member of the organisation.

What can I tell you about Eugenia? Our comrade was brave, she showed signs of great courage, of great political ability, of great leadership capacity. She had a total lack of interest in material possessions. For example, she once said to me: 'Look here, I've got this money inherited from my dad. Why don't we withdraw it and give it to the peasants?'

'You think we could?' I asked her.

'The crunch will come because my brothers want me to hand it over to them,' she told me. 'But there are some 10,000 *colones*[1] in all.'

It didn't bother her to drop her legal, above-board existence. It even made her happy to spend her entire time working for the revolution.

October, November and December 1976 were months covering a qualitative leap in the peasant labourers' movement.

---

[1] Worth about $4,000 in 1978

They'd drawn up their first Bill of Rights, in which they requested 9.50 *colones* a day [$1.50–$2]. They asked for a spoonful of rice, a spoonful of beans, a morsel of cheese and two *tortillas*. It ought to have come as news to the world to learn that people were still begging for food in our country. Their struggle for their rights was not just over a small wage increase, but over food and survival. It came as a shock.

This provided an impulse to the struggle. The landowners and oligarchs, seeing the movement develop, began to inflict repression.

In November our comrades organised a demonstration to publicise their bill in Quetzaltepeque. They came under attack from the city police and the national police. Simply by throwing stones they took the town hall. Something tremendous was taking place.

We were with the militant leadership of the FPL, in the peasant heartlands of the countryside. These were tremendous days for Javier, Eugenia and the other cadres there, days filled with hard work. We continued evaluating and giving direction to the situation, because we had no great experience of strikes, then paralysing the coffee and cotton plantations. There's been little experience of rural strikes in El Salvador. The strikes spread to a national level, and we were attempting to fill the gaps in our experience with daily lessons rooted in our organisation's political line, but above all basing ourselves solidly in the experience of the agricultural workers and of those cadres who, like Eugenia, had lived together with them, and worked intimately with them.

As a leader, Eugenia had a inner strength and a brilliant style. On the one hand she had acquired the knowledge of how to combine several activities and on the other she continued the task of expanding the movement, without losing herself in it all. She was a comrade endowed with a strategist's mentality and with methods to match. She never lost direction. She used to say: 'This is what happened, now let's take a look. This is the leadership executive's position. These are the plans for political education. Here are the new bases we're building, and all we possess are lists of contacts who've left behind the strikers on an agricultural estate and are now scattered over the rest of the country so we have to go to their aid.'

At the same time we were receiving information that we were going in the struggle for rights on that estate itself. She used to say: 'Our friends out there, we have to know how to organise

71

them.' She thought ahead, she considered things retrospectively, she looked at both sides and into the heart of things. She issued her memos in a calm style and in a looped handwriting, exquisite, on sheets of paper as large as this, very neatly written. She didn't use a typewriter because there wasn't one around. Eugenia's handwriting was itself impressive in the ways that her character was: smooth, rounded and clear.

Throughout all this period and in the midst of the chaos in which we were living, we went from one contact to another, we had no infrastructure, meaning we had no physical bases. So we began seeking support from among the people, but there were occasions when we couldn't use the phone, and Eugenia would be going round and round in the car for three hours, in order to hold the meeting. She'd pour out the news and I'd be taking notes asking: Look here, what about this? About that? And what about the other?

It was the same for Javier. She kept deepening her relationship with him as a comrade. They reached the point where it was possible to develop as individuals in greater companionship.

At the end of 1976 a problem surfaced that threatened to compromise Javier's safety. It additionally threatened Eugenia's, given that they'd come out in public as a couple. The organisation decided that there was no alternative but to send them into hiding. They had a brief space of time before this was due to happen, and they took advantage of it to get married. It fell to Isabel to explain to Eugenia what it meant to go underground and to prepare her for this significant step. Isabel continued:

I made contact with our comrade, and began to describe to her what it meant to be going into hiding.

'You,' I told her, 'will leave your family, your friends, and it's inevitable that some of your loved ones will die. Perhaps they'll kidnap your relatives to test if this'll lead them to you. You won't be able to do anything about it. You'll even see people you know in the street, and your heart will be in your mouth with the desire simply to say hello, but you won't be able to. You'll have to pass by on the other side. Perhaps they'll think, "How stuck up Eugenia's become" and you won't be able to turn and look at them and that'll hurt you.'

Eugenia didn't say anything, but began to cry. So I asked her: 'Are you ready?'

'Yes,' she answered.

'Why are you crying?'

'I *am* ready, but what you say hurts me. D'you know what hurts me most?'

'What?'

'That I won't be able to stay with the other comrades, as I have until now. All my worker comrades will be left believing absolutely anything, even that I may have betrayed them, and I don't know what else.' This is what affected her most deeply.

'Look here,' I told her. 'That's something they'd never believe. Don't let yourself worry on that account, because those comrades are the ones who'll see things as they really are, even without being told. They'll be super-clear in their own minds that you wouldn't have simply walked out, that you're away but continuing the struggle elsewhere.'

They left. They got married. I went to collect them and I met up with Javier first. Then I went together with him to fetch Eugenia. We obtained a house where we could all live together. I spent most of my time there, and worked alongside her.

Eugenia developed her political ideology more and more, along with her ability to make plans, her security techniques, her conviction. She started carrying out a large number of armed operations with an extraordinary serenity. Serenity doesn't imply a lack of fear. We talked this over together and she told me: 'Anyone who tells you he isn't afraid is telling lies. How could you not live in fear? The point is to overcome it.'

Eugenia was used to a very simple lifestyle; but living in secrecy she was obliged to wear a certain type of clothes, to wear make-up and high heels. That all took its toll, it's not easy.

The areas she took responsibility for began to develop at great speed. She succeeded in sowing the seeds of love and revolutionary enthusiasm in her comrades. She was very responsible about her work. There was no task she'd leave until the next day. It would be two in the morning, and Eugenia would still be writing away, doing her accounts, going over the filing, writing directives, stuffing envelopes to pass on to the next contacts. And at the same time she had to take care of washing and ironing her clothes, doing the cooking at the house, fulfilling all the tasks necessary to a domestic collective. And going on sentry duty whenever it was her turn.

From here she was transferred to a collective under Javier's command. It was a leadership collective. Our network had already been developed and by 1977 we had support teams of substantial capacity. In my own case, I worked directly within a cell, but hardly visited secondary collectives. She was in a secondary collective, a level immediately adjacent to my own.

Latterly, our comrade went on to submit an application requesting that she be proposed as a prospective member of the FPL. She'd sailed through incredibly easily.

Eugenia was physically weak, she always had asthma, and suffered from colds and allergies, in other words she was highly susceptible. Neither physical pain nor that caused by emotional difficulties ever sapped Eugenia's spirit. That's what impressed us. She never, never gave in. There's not a single instance one can point to and say, that's where Eugenia slipped up or got stuck. Eugenia was always in the vanguard.

The day came when we proposed her membership, along with that of several other comrades. She underwent a politico-military course and at the end of it she took her oath. It was on this occasion that Comrade Justo Mejía was also due to be sworn in. We were all deeply affected by his death. Four comrades remained to take the oath.

I remember the standard being raised, that the arms we'd used on the course were presented, and the comrades still didn't quite know what was going to happen. Of course they knew they'd submitted their applications and all that; we'd all been on the course and talked a lot of things through.

Throughout the course we'd assessed Eugenia's political, moral and ideological development. I remember Eugenia trembling. She trembled with emotion. Each one of them took the oath. In a firm voice she pronounced: 'I swear.'

The swearing-in read: 'Comrades: the FPL has received your applications to be members of this organisation. You know that the FPL defends the interests of the working class and of the people and whoever is committed to these aims must be ready to defend them as the most important undertaking in their life.'

'Comrades,' we told them, 'do you swear to remain faithful to the interests of the working class and of the people, and to defend them with your own life or that of someone dear to you?'

'I swear,' they each replied.

Then we asked them if they swore always to remain on the side of the poor and humble, loyal to them and never to oppose them. The comrades took the oath.

We asked them if they wanted to remain faithful to the FPL and bear the slogan 'Revolution or Death' with honour, in the conviction that the people in arms would attain victory.

'I swear,' they said.

Then we told them that if they did so the people would reward them and that if they did not, the people would call them to account. We went round each in turn, and as Justo Mejía had been killed and it was necessary to take the oath together, we said: 'Justo is dead but he lives in you. You will swear for Justo.' We all began to take the oath in unison.

'Comrade Justo Mejía,' we said, 'do you swear this and this and this?'

'I swear,' the four repeated.

So it was that Eugenia took the oath for herself and for Justo.

A few weeks later I was transferred away from the area. They put me on to military work. Ever since 1978, I've worked out in the military field.

Before all this, they asked who could be promoted from the agricultual workers' subcommittee to the Committee of the Masses, and Eugenia was proposed. She had the calibre, she was a cadre.

Earlier on, Eugenia had transferred to another cell. They were asking for cadres to lead the northern zone at the beginning of 1978. This was her proper niche. We didn't see her fulfilling her vocation within the subcommittee, we saw her more as a party worker, utilising her organisational capacity. She was proposed to take responsibility as a member of the leadership, a regional organiser. She was promoted to this. She had grown and succeeded in attaining leadership cadre within the organisation.

When we separated she was already pregnant. About a year later I saw her again together with Javier. We were given a dispensation to meet; the organisation knew we were as close as sisters.

Afterwards, through conversations with comrades, I learnt of her work in the northern zone. She continued as an example of the qualities she'd demonstrated during her time with us. On each occasion, of course, she seemed more mature. Eugenia never stagnated, never stayed the same. She was always in a process of unfolding.

Eugenia always lived for the future. That's the truth of it. Eugenia always lived for the future, and that's how she asked the rest of us to live.

Four

Eugenia and Javier began their clandestine existence just a few months before the presidential elections of 20 February 1977.

The 'official' PCN (Party of National Conciliation) candidate was General Carlos Humberto Romero, the Defence Minister under Molina and the architect of the repressive campaign of the last five years.

For its part, the UNO (National Union of Opposition) elected a liberal member of the military, Colonel Ernesto Claramount, as the opposition candidate.

On this occasion, electoral fraud surpassed that even of 1972, 1974 and 1976.

On 26 February the Central Electoral Committee announced that General Carlos Humberto Romero had won a crushing victory over Colonel Ernesto Claramount, with 812,281 votes to 394,661. According to well-documented evidence at UNO, the fraud was perfectly orchestrated, thanks to the direct collusion of the government, army, police and the ORDEN group along with members of the Central Electoral Committee itself. The principal methods used were the following: the duplication of names and addition of completely fictitious names to the electoral roll; the stuffing of ballot boxes with PCN votes before and during election day; the intimidation and violence used against voters at the voting tables by military and paramilitary officers; the expulsion, even the assault and arrest of UNO representatives legally present at the voting. They were also denied the right to be present at the vote-counting. The entire operation was coordinated by radio-controlled units. One of the proofs presented by the UNO to the US Congress was a tape of six

A large number of demonstrations took place in the Plaza de la Libertad in San Salvador, and Colonel Claramount announced that he would remain in the square until the Electoral Committee annulled the election results. Several thousand people kept him company. On 27 February, the Sunday, Father Alfonso Navarro, a Salvadorean Jesuit, offered Mass in the square before some 60,000 people. After the Mass, tanks, troops and the police surrounded the square, and the army ordered the demonstration to disperse. They threw tear-gas grenades and the people sought refuge in the El Rosario church. The government served Colonel Claramount with an ultimatum, and he found himself obliged to leave for Costa Rica, along with other UNO leaders.

The crowds reassembled the next day and government troops opened fire, killing around 200 demonstrators. The government officially acknowledged only eight deaths.

The oligarchs' official campaign against the Catholic Church had begun before the elections. The ultra-right singled out the Christian communities that had formed in various parts of the country as subversives and communists, apportioning particular blame to the Jesuits. On 11 December the army had occupied Aguilares and El Paisnal, Father Rutilio Grande's parish, and from then on the government began to expel foreign priests and to threaten, arrest and even torture Salvadorean ones.

Monsignor Oscar Arnulfo Romero became Archbishop of San Salvador on 22 February 1977, two days after the election of his namesake, General Romero. He had the blessing of the ruling oligarchy who never suspected he'd go over to the side of the poor and dispossessed.

On 12 March Father Rutilio Grande was assassinated, along with two peasants, while on his way to say Mass at El Paisnal. Archbishop Romero closed all Catholic schools and colleges for three days and cancelled all religious services for

---

[1] *El Salvador, un pueblo martirizado*, ed. IEPALA (Madrid, 1977), p. 16.

the following Sunday, permitting only a funeral Mass celebrated in front of a crowd of 100,000 people.

Persecution of the Church increased with further arrests, tortures and expulsions. On 11 May Father Alfonso Navarro was assassinated. He was the priest who said Mass in the Plaza de la Libertad, following February's fraudulent elections.

On 20 July the Union of White Warriors (UGB) issued an ultimatum to the 47 Jesuits still in the country, pressurising them to leave El Salvador immediately. The UGB's communiqué made the distinction that they were not persecuting the Church but only 'Jesuit terrorism'.

It was in these circumstances that General Romero was sworn in as president on 1 July 1977. Archbishop Romero refused to attend the ceremony.

President Carter had arrived at the White House in January 1977, boasting of his new campaign in favour of world human rights. General Romero was the first Latin American president to obtain power following Carter's election. The US Congress set up a committee to study the dreadful record of systematic violations of human rights in El Salvador and other Latin American countries.

To placate worldwide criticism, General Romero offered official protection to the Jesuits, which meant issuing orders to members of the security forces disguised as civilians not to carry out their threats. The official variety of terrorism abated slightly for a short interval, until Frank J. Devine was named US ambassador to El Salvador and the International Development Bank unblocked a new loan of $90 million which had been held back.

The assassination of a Salvadorean industrialist, Raúl Molinos Cañas, on 12 November 1977 gave Romero his pretext for returning to his iron-fisted policies. On 24 November the legislature approved the Defence and Guarantee of Public Order Law, a law aimed at the institutionalisation of the systematic violation of human rights in El Salvador. It was so flagrantly anti-constitutional that it was necessary to repeal it on 28 February 1978. In spite of this, institutionalised terror continued to gain strength.

'We decided to get married in the spring of '77,' Javier continued his story. 'We lived our life in hiding together. This was pretty painful to Eugenia. It didn't come naturally for her to abandon an open way of life among the people. It was hard going, contrary to what many who idealise life in hiding seem to think.'

'Javier's family is well-to-do,' María Elena de Girón recounted. 'His mother belonged to Opus Dei. His brothers were pretty right-wing but at all times expressed considerable solidarity with Javier. Eugenia and Javier worked together in Aguilares. It was there that FECCAS began its life as a revolutionary organisation.'

María Elena knew Javier when he was on the point of leaving university. A friend of both of them, she was one of the few people who attended their wedding. She recalled:

We arrived in a minibus with a group of women comrades. It was a wonderful moment, to be able to act as witnesses on such an occasion, especially for those of us who loved Eugenia. There were many friends who wished they could have come, according to what they told me. The wedding was an emotional event. They were married by a Spanish priest already highly involved in the popular struggle. The wedding was their initiation into a clandestine way of life. We could all feel it.

It was a beautiful ceremony, but when the betrothed couple made their vows, some of the guests left the church in protest because their vows included the promise to keep helping the people. Afterwards there followed a reception, a very lovely one, in the community hall of one of the churches. Even caviar was laid on. Javier and Eugenia danced and danced. I'd never seen them dance so much. They were happy.

The lovers said their goodbyes at the door. I embraced Eugenia. It was really a farewell. She cried and it made a very emotional scene. I had a presentiment that she would be going underground, and that I would never see her again, and so it turned out.

'One of the great drawbacks', Javier continued, 'of our secret existence was it cut across personal relationships. Above all for a militant like Eugenia, who had thousands of friends. She took it as one indispensable step towards her

79

contribution to the revolution, and specifically to the FPL, in order to lend it more weight. So her life in secrecy began in 1977 and lasted until her death.'

'Tell me something of a couple's life underground,' I asked him.

The whole situation surrounding the birth of our love sprang not only from a mutual liking but also from a close sharing of values. Our way of relating to the people, the worries we'd had ever since 1974, ultimately the whole development of our involvement in the revolutionary struggle as part of our people's liberation. All this we had in common. In addition, they were values that deepened as we met with field labourers, above all in our early years together. This meant that our relationship did not only jell from its inception, but that it developed very deeply. When we decided to marry, we experienced a real love, and from then on we lived that marriage with the stamp of our people's revolution upon it, and with the clear belief that the fundamental value for the two of us was the people, and linked to that our militancy within the FPL.

The step into secrecy obliged us to opt for a path that we couldn't count on being able to tread together the whole time. We could foresee the risks and the possibility of one of us losing the other.

It was something we were very conscious of from the start. We talked it over a lot, as we also discussed the question of children and whether or not to have them. Although both of us were very happy with the idea that our love should bear fruit, we decided that we wouldn't have a child during our first year of hiding, because we couldn't anticipate what it'd be like. Our lives had always been completely public at the heart of the mass movement.

We lived together during our first two years in hiding. Relatively together, since our revolutionary tasks were different ones. All the same, we considered that the step taken with our going into hiding was an important stage in our revolutionary life and in our love itself, in the development of our relationship.

Commander Nadia Palacios knew Eugenia before her active militancy in the FPL. She met her after her wedding and her immersion into her clandestine existence. Both women were militants in the same organisation. Nadia told me:

I knew Eugenia in 1968. I was a pupil at the Sacred Heart Convent School and she at another similarly bourgeois institution, that of the Assumption. We were active in a Catholic organisation which was developing activities in the poorest sectors. Eugenia was always characterised by her self-discipline and commitment to the people. This was obvious from her very real sacrifices before becoming involved in the revolution.

I lost sight of her. Because of the increased repression in the country, we both went into hiding and didn't meet up again until 1975, when I was myself head of the clandestine movement.

The qualities that Eugenia already possessed had been greatly developed. She had a considerable capacity for theoretical discussion, an impressive range of thought. She was deeply caught up in her work. If called upon, she would be in Chalatenango, in San Vicente, in Santa Ana. She travelled the whole country to carry out her work.

One thing I admired a lot, given that she had not only attended a bourgeois school but came from a bourgeois background, was that she never encountered communication failures with the peasants among whom she mainly worked. The male comrades treated her as one of the gang, only with a particular affection because she was such a tender-hearted comrade, such a committed one. She never hesitated to take up the tasks the organisation entrusted her with, however far away it might mean her going.

As regards her humility, I'll give you an example. When I worked in our organisation's cadre school, she was one of the instructors. It fell to her to give a talk about the party and its construction. It so happened that the organisation was questioning a number of points. She put forward an erroneous concept and her students used their cadre status to contradict her. Eugenia tried to argue against them and finally excused herself and explained that she would seek advice in the matter.

The school's directorship subsequently invited her to study the problem and she, in all humility, accepted the criticisms and agreed to repeat the talk with a critique of her own previous position, showing the cadres how, clearly, she had been mistaken.

As of 1975, effectively, and throughout all those years, I maintained a friendship with our comrade.

Javier remembered:

Eugenia accomplished her first armed action, a propagandist one, in May 1977. The operation involved a place near San Salvador. I remember it well because I led it.

She always had high hopes of participating directly, but she hadn't yet had the opportunity within the tasks so far allocated to her. This was a practical illustration of a whole campaign of armed propaganda undertaken by the organisation. The cell in which she operated developed a number of such armed propaganda campaigns.

The first was in the city of Apopa, in the bus terminal there. The situation was hardly a straightforward one, but she, ever since being told she had a part to play, seized upon it with great enthusiasm. She always applied herself closely to planning the whole operation.

It's true the operation didn't work out the first time. A fiesta was taking place exactly opposite where we were going to set it up. Because all the people were outside we had to suspend it. We put it off for two days.

Eugenia was in charge of security during the operation. It had all the significance of a military baptism for her. I remember we got back around three in the morning. We weren't able to talk or anything. The whole thing made quite an impression on her, in the sense that it implanted the desire to enlist in her, to face the armed struggle and the consequences of war. It was very important, despite the fact that at this time and for a long time afterwards she would continue working within a political framework.

Commander Ricardo also stressed this process of growing maturity that transformed Eugenia, a girl of bourgeois origins, into a militant revolutionary.

Our comrade was putting her energies into work in the northern zone for a long time. Her fundamental contribution was to the agricultural workers, but she was also extremely concerned with the incorporation of the working class.

Another basic question that was preoccupying her during her work there, was that of her military contribution while in that organisational cell. She accurately assessed the level of military development the zone needed to advance overall. At the same time, she was obliged to comply with a number of military targets.

Recently the organisation had used her primarily within its

political structure. Eugenia was herself a determining force in defining her party work. She was endowed with great organisational ability.

After many months in hiding [Javier recalled], the question of a baby surfaced again, along the lines that, under the circumstances, it would be very difficult to have one. We began to go more deeply into the risks and implications. There was substantial anxiety on both sides about having a child. It wasn't simply a matter of giving birth, but of taking on board the child's education and development under understandably difficult circumstances. The boy or girl would have to live in a safe house, subject to the risks, the sudden death of a parent, etc.

After nearly two years in hiding we decided to go ahead. By then we had undergone a lengthy process of extrapolating every possible implication. We were both experiencing an overwhelming desire for a child. Eugenia had her own highly individual opinion of what motherhood would mean to her. One of the things she most often returned to was the idea of any child of ours also belonging to the organisation and this filled her with happiness. She or he would simultaneously be the child of all the comrades with whom we most closely shared the changing fortunes of war.

In this sense, she had great confidence that the organisation would take responsibility in the event of either of us dying. Eugenia was already in a position which entailed very heavy work duties. Before finalising her decision about becoming pregnant she obtained a medical check-up and it emerged that she was suffering from acute anaemia.

The doctor recommended that she shouldn't become pregnant for at least three months. This must have been in July 1978. Before the critical three months could elapse I was captured, having fallen into enemy hands.

The National Guard caught Javier, along with Eugenia's sister Marta and some other comrades, in a security raid in the outskirts of San Salvador on 16 October 1978. Marta was then nine months pregnant. What follows is her own account of her abduction and the treatment meted out to her in prison and then in hospital.

We were seized and taken to prison, and each of us was provided with a cover story. I recited mine to the enemy. I said I was out looking for a child-minder because I was about to have a baby, and I went into this house to see one, and I'd fainted there and was confused and didn't know anybody.

Then they beat me. When they seized us, they threw us face down onto the floor. Then, when they blindfolded us and bundled us into the truck, I began to yell. They took me along in a different car because I couldn't get up on to the big lorry.

I began to yell so that the news should spread through our district and shouted my mum's phone number. From then on I didn't speak again until we reached the guards' barracks. They began to ask me details, and lifted up my clothes. They ran their hands all over me, belly and all. They said: 'Now we'll fetch the blade, don't worry, this kid'll get delivered here and now, and there's already a heap of fathers ready for him, and he'll go on to have many more.' They threatened me with rape, but there was one who attempted to win me over in order to make me talk.

They forced each of us into separate cells. They threw me in one too, then went down the line hitting us. They beat my back with a rifle butt. I started going into labour, but didn't say anything about it to them.

They had me stretched out on a bed and I couldn't stand the labour pains any longer. I could feel the contractions, but as I was blindfolded I couldn't tell if there were people there with me. I could only try to listen. Then they noticed I was in pain and ordered me to start 'singing'. I told them I didn't know anything. They kept on trying to make me talk.

Then they told me they were going to take me out. I assumed they meant to torture me, but they put me in an ambulance and told me they were going to take me to hospital.

It so happened that that day I'd just been to the doctor and when they searched my handbag they found his name and the confirmation that I was nine months' pregnant. I didn't have to say anything for them to see for themselves. They took me to the maternity hospital and had me admitted under a different name, a major manoeuvre. When I interposed my real name they hushed me up, put me in a room and changed my name to another one.

As I sat there, quantities of people were arriving for the maternity ward. They began to undress me in order to get me into the hospital smock and I gave them my real name, and asked them to let my mum know where I was. They passed the message on, but when she came in search of me, she was told that no one of my name had been admitted. They'd kept me under the false one. I was considered 'disappeared' until two days later when someone I knew recognised me.

The enemy never guessed that, thanks to my family, I would know so many people. They thought they'd got me completely isolated, that I'd give birth within the 24 hours, then they'd snatch me back, stick the baby into an orphanage and me into jail. What saved me was that when I'd started shouting that I was in under a false name, that I wasn't really called that, although some of the nurses wouldn't believe me, one of the employees called my mum.

Then a doctor arrived, took a look and recognised me from my family resemblance. I told him I belonged to such-and-such a family. 'It's true,' he told the nurses, 'she looks the part.'

'I can't do a lot for you because the man in charge here is in with the Guard and goes along with what they want,' he told me. 'But I'll help you as much as I can, don't worry.'

He gave me a Caesarean section, so delaying my departure by another week. He never said this was the reason, but I figure it was, in order to protect me. He advised the doctor in charge: 'She can't give birth normally. We have to operate.'

The guards on duty created a commotion because they wanted to gain admission to the operating theatre with me. They did get in. As I came round, they interrogated me. I was completely stupefied from the anaesthetic.

Thanks to hospital employees, my husband found out where I was. He came to look for me but was informed I wasn't there. He was also an activist. They put me into a remote room, cut off from all the other patients. No one knew, because I wasn't in any of the regular wards. The hospital manager arrived to try and get me to talk, saying that nothing would happen to me.

On the third day they tried to take my baby away, to remove him to the orphanage and to get me out. The hospital staff behaved magnificently. They invented a case of anaemia for me, an infection that would detain me and give my family time to find me.

'How long were you a prisoner there?' I asked Marta.

'About a week. I left for my mum's house and stayed with her for a month or so. I took the baby with me.'

'At this time I was working with students,' said Ondina, the younger sister. 'When they rang the house, I took one of the calls. I began to put the word out among our comrades and so forth, but what probably helped Marta most was that she managed to smuggle out a note. The nurse, very conscious of what she was doing, took her to the bathroom so that my mum could see her. She had a great sense of solidarity.'

Thanks to this solidarity on the part of the doctor and nurses, Marta's mother was warned and could save her daughter and her newborn grandson from the sinister destiny accorded to the Salvadorean 'disappeared'.

'The note Marta smuggled out of the hospital with one of the nurses,' Ondina continued, 'proved decisive in saving Javier's life and that of the other abducted comrades. The scrap of paper listed their names and the address where they were being held. The government forces had no alternative but to acknowledge their existence as prisoners and to hand them over to the courts.'

Javier said:

Four months went by from the time of my kidnap until we could meet. I spent the first two weeks at the National Guard headquarters. I was subjected to every form of torture. D'Abuisson personally oversaw it all.[1]

This stage left a profound impression on us. Our relationship grew dramatically in intensity. We each equally lived the daily experience of living so close not only to the possibility but also to the reality of a separation forced upon us by the enemy.

At the very beginning, I thought I'd never get out, and Eugenia also believed as much. For the first fortnight I was totally 'disappeared'. After ten days without any news at all, although she said that deep down she never entirely lost hope, Eugenia thought she'd probably never see me again.

I remember the first little note to reach me in jail, after the fortnight spent at Santa Tecla prison under court orders. She told me that one of the greatest sufferings she had to undergo was that of not having become pregnant. That was the opening sentence of her letter.

This was perhaps a turning-point in Eugenia's life. She often

---

[1] Following the 'free elections' of 28 March 1982, Roberto D'Abuisson, a former major in the security forces, was elected president of El Salvador's constituent assembly.

repeated that her three dearest concerns were her people, the organisation and myself. Our relationship synthesised her entire life. On receiving the news of my abduction, she went through a process of serious reflection. It was possible to reconstruct it once we were together once more. She said she never would have believed it possible to experience such a searing pain as she did on believing me to be lost to her. This helped her to see how far our relationship had progressed. She had not been through such acute pain since her father's death. She added that it was probably the sharper, due to her level of political awareness.

Eugenia overcame her pain, converting it into an intensification of her work. She used it to accomplish her tasks as a revolutionary more fully, given the impossibility, for security reasons, of expressing the pain she was going through. It was a heavy load to bear.

I think it must have been a period when our comrade gained greatly in her proletarian understanding. The organisation plainly perceived Eugenia's new level of development. Those comrades I succeeded in looking up later and who worked with her through this time were very impressed by this. They said that not only did Eugenia know how to overcome her pain, but that she also managed to convert it into fresh energy to apply to her work.

Then another highly significant event occurred, when I left the jail in February 1979 and we met for the first time in more than four months. The new reunion was endowed with the same industry as the former separation, but was of a very different order.

Eugenia's stoicism, the redirection of her pain when faced with her husband's abduction, made her the object of admiration among her companions at work, and led me to ask Javier, 'What was Eugenia's attitude to sexual equality within the revolutionary struggle?' He answered:

The women's liberation movement was never a problem for her. In her relations -- as a woman -- with the outside world, in her revolutionary development, in her relationship with me, Eugenia always fought all traces of the *machismo* she had come across in her comrades, including the women. Eugenia maintained that it was through involving our people in the revolutionary struggle that women would liberate themselves, obtaining their true and fair place.

She said that three important factors had been instrumental in her development as a woman: the discovery of her people, the suffering of her people, and the liberation struggle of her people, into which she'd incorporated herself.

She had a sincere love for the FPL. Her revolutionary militancy, her political militancy, were both deeply linked with her personal development as a woman. That led her to discover a series of values she had to integrate – her relationship with me as a comrade and as a wife.

She was always very critical of any traces of surviving *machismo*, for example over the division of labour and what were assumed to be women's chores and what men's. She responded very strongly to these issues. For example, she'd get highly annoyed when men tried to smoothe the way for the women comrades on long marches, or when performing revolutionary duties.

Once, in December 1976, we made a long trek with our comrade workers from the countryside. Fifteen of us went. The trek was unforeseen, and Eugenia was wearing sandals. Her toes got scraped, and she continued with bleeding feet. When our comrades noticed this, they at first suggested constructing a stretcher, then that we should take turns in carrying her. Eugenia stopped, and told them that she had not observed a comparable response in similar situations with male sufferers, that we were reacting in that manner because of her gender, that we were making her into an object of pity, and that she considered she had the capacity and the duty to carry on, and not to make a nuisance of herself.

Because the load was a very heavy one, we were carrying it in relays. When it came to her turn, a comrade offered to take it for her. Eugenia, who could be rude, reacted violently. 'Like shit you will,' she informed him. It was in her behaviour that one could see the ways in which she demanded equal treatment for men and women.

I remember many of the great leaders who played a part in forming the pair of us. Polín, for example, was like a brother to her. He always asserted that the Salvadorean peasant had strong vestiges of *machismo* and that Eugenia, in terms of her relationship with them, had succeeded in communicating a more critical approach to all such traits.

'What did Eugenia think of women's liberation?' I asked Marta. She answered:

About women's liberation, I'm not so sure. The way we talked about it always took as its starting point that women had a part to play in society, and secondly that she had to play an active part over the issue of equal rights. This we'd known within the family, in growing up with brothers. She'd demonstrated she had the same ability as them.

When my father died, it was she who took up the reins. More so than our eldest brother. She used to say a matriarchy ruled in the home. My brothers agreed that it was a matriarchy because we had an inclination to dominate and it was we who wanted to take up the reins.

As far as our comrades in the countryside were concerned, Eugenia had the same formation as me in the forging of peasant cadres. She was responsible for creating a multitude of militants. Eugenia always told them they had to rid themselves of their *machismo* and treat their wives on equal terms, they had to share the chores, etc. Without issuing documents, she contributed practical work towards achieving women's equality with their comrades.

There was something else she did towards helping a group of peasant women in the countryside to raise their consciousness. She gave them talks on the subject of *machismo*, and promoted their participation. The male comrades accused us of 'inciting' the women.

When women were included in the agrarian organisation, they were accepted on equal terms. This was thanks to the work of the organisation as the giver of principles, and also thanks to the women comrades we recruited in the countryside. Eugenia was an example and a prime mover.

Five

There exist innumerable instances in which the heroism of Salvadorean women stands out. For every one that's public knowledge, there are many more that go unrecorded because all the witnessses are dead.

Nélida Anaya Montes, Commander Ana María, told me the story of a primary school mistress who was called Inés Dimas. Inés had been decorated with the Santiago Ibarbarena medal for Tutorial Merit by the National Assembly: a distinction greatly coveted by members of ANDES, the Salvadorean union of teachers and tutors.

Inés was active in the Farabundo Martí brigade of the FPL. She was forty-three.

If you came face to face with this woman, you would consider her nervous. I knew her intimately throughout twelve years of struggle together. Anyone simply meeting up with her would never believe she had such a constitution and courage. The comrades used to say that Inés was always in the right place at the right time, wherever she was needed.

Then when she went underground all the teachers were asking after Inesita. They assumed something was up, but they also missed her a lot. She was adored by the children, by the teachers, by everyone.

Then a very serious incident occurred. Members of our organisation had met together when a bomb exploded just in front of them, an enormous bomb that destroyed the house. So the crisis meant we had to evacuate the area; and, to cap it all, we had a printing press in the house. Inés was in there with one other woman comrade when Comrade Marcial succeeded in gaining access. Inesita had tidied everything away, so this woman, who gave the appearance of being so highly-strung – the area was teeming with police – do you know what she did? She went out and bought *tamales*,[1] made coffee, offered it to the guards and made small-talk with them, chatting on with such gems as: 'Oh dear, you do have a hard time of it', making it seem as if she were with them all the way.

The next day, without more ado, she quit the house. She never aroused the least suspicion. That showed us her calibre.

A North American journalist called Ann Nelson was there at Inesita's death and later described it in a radio commentary made in New York. What follows is her account:

After two weeks in El Salvador (I was put up in a house rented by a group of international journalists near the US embassy), I was returning home when I heard the sound of gunfire in the street. There were armoured cars the length of the block, and some 50 National Guardsmen and police. They were armed with mortars, machine-guns, and a tank, and were attacking a private house. What was unbelievable was that the entire onslaught was being launched against a single house and the only shots one could hear coming from indoors were coming from a hand pistol. In contrast, there was a whole army there outside, with plain-clothes officers manning the machine-guns.

The small-arms fire ceased to be heard. Everything fell silent.

The smoke began to disperse and the first group of police and journalists went into the house. There was a young woman, maybe 25 years old, dead in the bath. There was also a woman aged about 40 to 45, wearing a pinafore and with a headscarf on, stretched out in a pool of blood. Her death appeared to have been caused by a grenade. There was a girl of about 17 or 18, also in a pool of blood. And a duplicator close by.

It was a publicity centre for the FPL and contained a load of propaganda posters and leaflets which said: 'We must educate the people, we must reach out to the people.' All these were strewn around by the guards in order to impress the journalists.

I was the only woman in the group and the only North American journalist who'd stayed for more than a couple of days in the course of a whole month in El Salvador.

---

[1] Maize pancakes, usually stuffed with beans or vegetables.

Then came the moment when I couldn't believe my eyes. The Chief of Police went into another room and got a machine-gun. He knelt beside the older woman and put it in her hand. 'This was the weapon, this was the machine-gun she was shooting at us with,' he said. He got a box of unused bullets, still in their paper wrappers, and threw them on the floor into her blood. 'Those were her bullets,' he said.

The international press and I, we were all witnesses. They kept taking photos, saying 'Right, right,' and taking notes: 'She had a machine-gun, she was firing on government forces . . . terrorist . . . guerrilla,' and so forth.

The Chief of Police repeated the process with the 17-year-old girl. He provided her with an Uzi or something of the kind, I'm not sure what, and also rolled the bullets into her blood.

On one of the walls somebody, I never knew if it was the residents of the house or the government security forces dressed in plain-clothes (sometimes described in the press as the right-wing 'death squads'), had written 'FPL' in letters of blood. I took pictures of all this, of the men inserting the rifles into the dead women's grasp and throwing the bullets on to the floor.

Ana María gave a concise account of the same event: 'There were three comrades. The house was surrounded. They had armoured cars, even helicopters. Despite the inequality of forces, the battle went on for half a day, until the house was completely destroyed. They hadn't dared to force an entry. What was beautiful, and instructive, was what they found when they finally entered: Inés, brought down by the bullets, but who had first managed to write FPL on the wall in her own blood. It was a gun-battle that made quite an impression in the capital city.'

I asked Ana María and then several more woman revolutionaries about the rôle of women in politico-military and grassroots organisations in El Salvador. From her position as second-in-command in the Farabundo Martí front of the FPL, in other words as Commander Marcial's deputy, Ana María could speak with considerable authority on the roots of women's problems within the Salvadorean revolution. What follows is in answer to my question:

According to one of its statutory principles, and not only from statutes but from practice, the FPL always propounded that women's participation in the revolution, and concretely within the organisation, should be given maximum influence. Women should be employed not merely in a supportive capacity, but as combatants and commanders, to afford them maximum support and ample space in which to develop.

Women's activity in all our organisations was high, but perhaps especially so in the FPL. In the FPL their contribution was substantial at all levels, as political militants, within leadership cells at intermediate and superior levels. For example, I was in a top-level cell.

The organisation provided all possible real and concrete conditions for women to develop according to their capacities and potential. They found their level according to what they could best fulfil.

Being a mother didn't present contradictions. The women comrades organised themselves in such a way that they were even able to say, fine, I'm going to leave my child in the care of my lover while I undertake revolutionary projects. There were instances when we came across one of these men, all thumbs, attempting to put on a nappy, because he regarded it as his task. We couldn't abolish *machismo* overnight, but it's on its way out.

Commander Nadia, also a militant within the Farabundo Martí front of the FPL, confirmed Ana María's words:

When the revolutionary organisations were first formed, there was no ideological discrimination between men and women. In the FPL the statutory principles were identical. But basic principles are one thing and a country's history another, a development that involves men and women from the time they're born. One was drawn into the struggle through this history.

The country was marked by its characteristic of involving the women in all forms of work. In the case of my organisation, in the Revolutionary Council, the highest level of leadership, 40 to 45 per cent of us were women. The Central Command had a similar percentage. Our second-in-command (Ana María) is a woman. There are several more women in the Political Committee, and if you go on down to the base organisations you'll find firing squad and squadron commanders, and grassroots and popular power leaders.

Women have certainly been accorded recognition, but this

doesn't mean that there still aren't differences in terms of the value accorded to the work of each gender at separate levels. It's a continual struggle one has to carry on without falling into erroneous positions of wishing to declare women superior to men; woman is exactly man's equal. One has to respect the equality of opportunities, duties and rights as part of the revolutionary process.

Equality between men and women is at the root of the bill of rights of the Democratic Revolutionary government. We women are 51 per cent of El Salvador's population.

Personally, I've not come across serious difficulties in involving myself in different sorts of revolutionary activity. The organisation favours women's participation as such. For example, there are no restrictions regarding motherhood, there are no contradictions imposed on us as a result of our personal and physical make-up.

'I haven't met with problems. On the contrary, where there are women there is more understanding and the work seems more cheerful. This is something even our male comrades can see, to such an extent that they themselves ask that there should be women in the majority of cells because, whether one likes it or not, they contribute a positive element of understanding and compassion lacking among the men who feel such things do not conform to their self-image.

Commander Mercedes del Carmen Letona belongs to another politico-military organisation, the People's Revolutionary Army (ERP). I asked her the same question about the difference in opportunities open to men and to women in the revolutionary struggle. Her reply, as we shall see, was similar to those provided by Ana María and Commander Nadia:

In terms of the struggle itself, there is no inequality of opportunity. And if we look a little at how the whole revolutionary movement grew and accelerated in the country, especially if we return a little further to the teachers' strikes and the mass movements of 1968 or 1971, we find that women's contribution is comparable.

Within that context there is a whole struggle for rights which, to the extent that it progressed by confronting oppression, gradually acquired political characteristics. Women began to take an equal part in terms of active military service. This was the process of development, of the upsurge in revolutionary organisations. In terms of their integration at higher levels of commitment, for example in the armed struggle, men and women's participation was an equal one within the country's revolutionary organisations. The relevant factor taken into account was the individual's capacity for assuming responsibility.

Talking of *machismo*, I had men under my command during the period we were creating the political and military cells. No problems resulted.

We believe that at this time women undoubtedly have to play a major part in every aspect of the life of this country – its political, social and economic life. Once victory has been gained, the question of oppression will no longer arise. Women will possess the opportunity to assert their claim to full participation, but until that day women have to struggle for the liberation of their people. Later, when they've broken these chains, women will have the opportunity to stake their own claim.

Every human being dreams of having a family. Even within a new situation, it's natural to still hope to bear children, to build a family, though a family unit is so difficult to achieve under present circumstances. It's something we often daren't even think about now, but which'll become possible in the future.'

In my interview with Eugenia's sisters, Marta and Ondina, I also raised the question of gender equality. 'Did your comrades acknowledge this equality?' I asked.

'Yes, they admitted to it,' Marta said. 'In addition, our menfolk shared the household chores. We came from families where men never lifted a finger. Our men are likewise of bourgeois extraction, but they had to change. The organisation changes you. They don't resent the fact that sometimes we have more important things to do.'

'My husband,' Ondina added, 'always says that duty comes first, even if that means I go out and he stays to do the washing. That's what happens with the vast majority of the male comrades in the organisation. Learning to wash clothes, cooking and cleaning, teaches you that these are also valid tasks. Someone has to be concerned with them.'

'Sometimes,' Marta said, 'I came across comrades who objected to minding the children. There's always an ideal system of collective labour, but there are cases, instances, in which the organisation as a party has to put more work into its staff.

'Women have to take part in constructing society. Oppressed women have to raise their heads. Women's integration has made great strides in the countryside. There are women front leaders, squadron leaders, some who are working for the party. I know many women comrades in positions of authority.

'This doesn't suit some of the peasants. The women comrades have had to confront them. Others have accepted the change. There is a substantial female involvement inside the FPL and, according to what I've been told, in other similar organisations. The problem centres on the children. What happens in the bases is that the old women mind the children. We even have ladies of over sixty who work in with us.'

'I worked in the slums,' said Ondina. 'There women's involvement was almost as extensive as men's. In those slums there were women comrades who were still young, and who had got stuck into the work. There were also ladies who were more valiant than the men. The Salvadorean woman is a great fighter. She dominates within the slums because she takes such an important part in the heaviest work, sometimes at five in the morning.'

'What did Eugenia think of the revolution as a liberating force?' I asked.

'What we discussed with Eugenia,' Marta replied, 'was our view that under capitalism woman was crushed, violated, usurped and that the only hope she had of attaining full womanhood was to become involved in the struggle for a new society, a socialist society. Women's liberation goes hand in hand with socialist victory.'

Six

Having a child is a small way of extending one's own life [Javier told me]. While I was a prisoner Eugenia vividly experienced the pain of not having become pregnant. On the other hand, our enforced separation made us grapple with our relationship once more in order to re-evaluate it. Our love deepened and consolidated, acquired a new dimension.

After four months of not seeing one another, our reunion was a deep experience, with the feeling of a victory. If I'd succeeded in getting out of jail, it was basically as a result of battles fought by the people, through the combination of the struggle on behalf of political prisoners launched by the mass organisations led by the BPR [Popular Revolutionary Bloc], and through international pressure. Those were the crucial factors in getting me out of enemy clutches in order to continue the struggle.

I lived with Eugenia for three weeks after I got out. The war situation rendered it impossible to meet her for the first few days. She seemed a lot more mature. Our desire to conceive a child was so strong that she became pregnant almost at once.

Our revolutionary commitments kept us from living together for the nine months of her pregnancy. At that time she was in the National Committee of the Masses under Central Command, and I was in the Popular Liberation Militias. We met up once a week, sometimes twice.

Eugenia lived her pregnancy to the fullest, every day. The two of us followed the baby's progress step by step, with help from our comrades and from books.

The first two months were very difficult: she was on the point of miscarrying. The doctor recommended a month of complete rest, but she felt unable to comply due to her revolutionary obligations. Her group forbade her to attend meetings, in order to force her to get some rest.

On one occasion, they were going to have an important

meeting in the house where she was living. Eugenia took her mattress into the room where they were all going to meet, put herself to bed and pretended to be asleep. The comrades came in and began their meeting. By the time they'd registered what was happening she was taking part in it.

Her passion for her work and the multiplicity of her projects made her seek all possible means of not abandoning them. She used to say that her pregnancy could not keep her from her duties, despite the attendant dangers; that she had to combine the problems of war with the problems of the pregnancy.

It was during the early months of Eugenia's pregnancy that the neighbouring country of Nicaragua reached the apotheosis of its long and arduous revolutionary process, which in so many respects parallels the Salvadorean one in which Eugenia and Javier were involved. The Sandinista National Liberation Front (FSLN) was formed in 1961 and started the long haul of clandestine struggle, of guerrilla incursions, of the gradual organisation of the masses and its social efforts against the dictatorial Somoza dynasty that had ruled the country without interruption since 1936.

In May 1979 what would be the FSLN's last offensive, and that of the whole Nicaraguan people, began to overthrow the Somoza empire and its fearful National Guard. There was a bloody struggle lasting approximately six weeks. It combined a general strike with national insurrection. With the convergence of numerous guerrilla columns on the capital (Managua), the Nicaraguan people – commanded by its vanguard the FSLN – toppled the dictatorship and seized revolutionary power on 19 July 1979.

'What political and psychological effect did the triumph of the Sandinista revolutionaries have on the revolutionary movement in El Salvador?' I asked Javier.

I wouldn't deny that the effect of the Sandinista victory on the Salvadorean revolutionary process was very important. It reinforced the whole revolutionary praxis in El Salvador, fundamentally as far as our organisation was concerned, and showed the possibility of a small, underdeveloped and economically dependent country routing a military dictatorship backed by the US, on the basis of its determination to struggle and by means of armed insurrection.

The Sandinista revolution again demonstrated that the people possess the ability to seize power by force of arms, to overthrow military dictatorship.

This inspired renewed confidence. It raised revolutionary awareness and spirit. It reinforced the revolutionary movement's aspirations for power. Psychologically, and in terms of morale among the people's combatants, among their leaders and organisations, it was very significant. The theory we'd been upholding was given a real-life demonstration in Nicaragua's example.

The political effect went the deepest, I believe. In the first place, I could see that a revolutionary process was underway in Central America, and that in its heart a revolution had already taken place on our doorstep. It shifted the balance throughout the region. The whole Central American revolutionary movement took a step forward with the Sandinista victory.

Eugenia worked in the FPL's clandestine cell throughout her pregnancy, with the responsibility for directing its work with the agricultural labourers. Alongside her, also in the network's directorate, was Apolinario (Polín) Serrano, a peasant by birth, and a few others. Polín, as his friends affectionately called him, was an outstanding revolutionary, one of the peasants closest to Archbishop Romero. His pseudonym, or *nom de guerre*, was Rogelio. Commander Nadia, who also knew him personally, described this comrade's career to us.

He was born in the Aguilares region, to the north of El Salvador, and enlisted in the peasant struggle. He was a man always deeply sensitive to the problems of his class. Because of this, and his Catholic upbringing, he reached the stage of becoming involved with FECCAS, and little by little there he began to shine as a real leader.

He became secretary-general of FECCAS without knowing how to read or write. He learned to read very well. Learning to write proved harder, for it required a manual dexterity he had never developed. He then became secretary-general of the FTC (FECCAS-UTC) and a member of the BPR's National Directory Executive.

He was an exemplary comrade in every respect. He overcame

a peasant mentality and adopted a proletarian system of thought and action.

Polín owned a little smallholding which he donated to FECCAS. He said that the only thing binding him to this private property was an element of backwardness in his consciousness. He turned himself into a real proletarian, and dedicated himself to revolutionary activities full-time. Once inside FECCAS he demonstrated not only organisational abilities but a capacity for analysis, an identification with revolutionary principles, a great honesty, and also intelligence in applying revolutionary techniques and theories of labour. Latterly this led him to incorporate himself in the ranks of the FPL. There the militancy that underlay his revolutionary impulse developed.

Within the FPL his development gathered momentum as his political vision grew, along with his military understanding of the war. He covered every type of undertaking with great efficiency. At a certain stage he was promoted to full membership. He was a member of our Revolutionary Council and was elected by the permanent leadership of the organisation, the Central Command. As member of the command he assumed a position of primary responsibility on the National Committee of the Masses. There he took over not only the leadership of work to be undertaken in the countryside, but also the organisation of agricultural workers, students, teachers, etc. He naturally rose to the top in every area of grassroots work.

His initiative in learning how to read and write was the consequence of his over-riding commitment to the revolution. Polín immediately put his new-found skill at the service of the revolutionary process. Later on he served as an instructor at our squadron training school.

He had an enormous gift for self-expression. He was very sensitive and very profound. He had a captivating manner of speaking and he knew how to phrase clear explanations. He was warmly applauded at meetings.

Within the Central Command he took over not only the leadership of the masses, but also showed an ability to relate the solutions to problems, whether of a political, logistic or military variety, to structural ones to do with the squadron. He had a very dynamic and effective presence overall. On occasions, he represented our organisation abroad. He served as FPL delegate on special missions and with considerable success. His theoretical development, his proletarianisation, didn't lead him to lose the awareness of his roots, a quality that went with his peasant identity.

Polín, in finding his way through the Christian communities, had many links with priests, nuns, the upper reaches of the Catholic hierarchy. He was closely in touch with Monsignor Romero as the direct result of those qualities I've just mentioned. He had a deep respect for the Church's principles. He took up a Marxist-Leninist position and always respected the people's religious beliefs, respected Church structures, placing himself simultaneously – and with all humility – in the position of believing in the necessity that the Church should work with the oppressed at all times. He greatly influenced Monsignor Romero in this respect.

He always came up with something to say to amuse us. On one occasion he was reading Marx and became highly excited. He called one of his comrades over and said: 'Look here, this old fellow ought to come and give a few lectures to us here.'

One proof of his spirit of self-sacrifice is in the resumés he presented to the Central Command. In order to win approbation from all the command members and in his desire for emulation, Polín presented the best possible memos and summaries of his work. To present his work so scrupulously he had to take considerable pains. No resumés had ever been presented with such clarity, thoroughness and comprehension.

He was thirty-four when he died and had spent about six years in the FPL. He gave over ten years to the struggle in the countryside, from FECCAS's inception. He died on 24 September 1979. He was going with two comrades from Santa Ana to San Salvador and was abducted close by the Cavalry Barracks. All the available evidence indicates that the government captured then massacred and buried them. The government attempted to make out that they had opened fire. That's ridiculous, something we'd always denounced as a crime. The enemy tipped the corpses into a pit. And that month Polín was going to be married.

'Polín's death along with the other comrades was a serious blow for us and our organisation,' Javier said.

Over half of Eugenia's cell was liquidated and she had to take on virtually all the work. With the death of our comrades our network was laid wide open and security problems arose. As always, Eugenia's reaction was to intensify her work. Once again she converted her anguish into an enormous energy, a driving force.

Her revolutionary stature also radiated from her in this period. It marked a watershed in her life as a militant that forced her to reach a new stage of maturity. Despite her pregnancy and the problems she'd had, she threw herself into rebuilding all her work, into remaking networks, into resolving security problems, which meant she had to go out to the countryside, trekking and so forth.

Polín and the two other comrades who died were inseparable friends: they were also close to us, had witnessed the deepening of our romance and knew Eugenia intimately.

Eugenia remained abreast of her commitments. There was one time when she admitted to me that the work and the physical stress were too strenuous. The possibility of a miscarriage recurred when she was already six months into her pregnancy. Yet she still explained how her priorities lay in the importance of her work and the deep sense of responsibility she had towards her people in the face of the hammering given the FPL. Although a miscarriage might have been the saddest thing in the world, underneath she had made the choice that if it couldn't be avoided, she could not desert her work for the sake of the infant. This, according to Eugenia, was something we had to accept.

Once more we went over the entire meaning of our revolutionary choice, how it was a commitment on the part of us both to uphold its principles and values. It was at times like those, hard ones humanly-speaking, that we reverted to fundamental choices.

The decision we'd gone for spelt out that she probably wouldn't miscarry, but that if it resulted from our fulfilment of revolutionary duty, it would be a fresh point to concede the enemy, a pain that on the one hand would be deepened by our love for our people and, on the other, class hatred.

There her revolutionary stature shone forth again. She carried on her work, increased the load by increasing her projects, and didn't miscarry. After she'd given birth to our child, she repeated how she'd 'demonstrated' that she was right all along, that she'd never believed she was going to miscarry.

In the midst of the chores connected with the reconstruction of the secret network, broken by the death of Polín and his comrades, the coup of 15 October 1979 occurred. The United States, reacting against the Sandinista victory in Nicaragua, gave their blessing to the coup that knocked the useless dictator General Romero from power and replaced him with a military junta composed of Colonels Arnoldo Majano and Jaime

Abdul Gutiérrez, who announced a reformist programme and invited various progressive figures to power-share in the Junta and in its ministries.

'What effects did the coup of 15 October have on your lives?' I asked Javier.

I don't think it had any serious repercussions, for two reasons. If you remember, the FPL was the only organisation to expose the 15 October coup as a manoeuvre of US imperialism, another card in its pack of counter-revolutionary strategies. Neither ourselves as individuals nor our organisation had any particular expectations of the coup or of what possible benefit might be derived.

The BPR took the same line. We said it was necessary to continue the struggle, to unmask the machinations of imperialism, that strategic piece of manoeuvering from the US. Neither the life of the organisation nor those of its members were of any real consequence. For us that stage of the war went on and it was politically important that the people understood that we were dealing with an example of imperialistic puppeteering. All our strategy and tactics were enlisted in this cause, in opposition to the opinions being advanced by other revolutionary organisations at this time. Later on, events demonstrated that our organisation's analysis and explanation were correct.

Eugenia and Javier continued in hiding. On 13 December 1979 Ana Patricia was born.

At that time I was engaged in military duties [Javier continued]. One day when I was in the mountains on a military course, I had the sudden urge to write a note to Eugenia. It coincided exactly with our daughter's birth.

Ana Patricia was born on a Thursday and I arrived on the Saturday to see her. It was the day that Eugenia came out of hospital. When I got home and went into the bedroom where our little girl lay, Eugenia wasn't there. She was rinsing out the baby's bottles in the kitchen.

She returned to her revolutionary tasks in under a week and resumed normal life in all other respects. She never for a moment neglected her duties, nor did she disregard the child. She not only provided her with a deep love but also began to impress certain ways of being upon her.

It needs to be stressed that Eugenia lived her whole pregnancy with great intensity, love and happiness. Our daughter's birth again gave us a qualitatively new impulse, opened up immense dimensions to our relationship, deepened the love between us in a very strong way, and – it goes without saying – laid new responsibilities at our door.

Three weeks after Ana Patricia's birth Javier completed his military course and returned to San Salvador. Although it was not possible for him to reside in the same house as Eugenia and the baby, they shared a close relationship and he was fully involved in his daughter's daily life.

It was necessary to combine the care of our daughter with our revolutionary obligations. From the beginning Eugenia was concerned that we should both share the chores connected with Ana Patricia. She had a very clear idea that both parents should split every aspect of childcare – broken nights, nappies, the lot.

So her existence as a mother began. Within months – within days – the baby started attending meetings, and began to criss-cross the country, sometimes with her mum, sometimes with me. Within reason, rather than leave her with other comrades, we took the responsibility ourselves even though it made the going harder.

In April 1980 Eugenia was made a member of the Organisational Committee in the Central Command. This committee's basic responsibility was to building the party, and the political and organic development of the organisation's party structures, allowing for the guidance of the popular masses and armed units into guerrilla activity, the armed forces and the militias.

Our hardest task was to discover the type of party we had to construct in order to advance the revolutionary process and to do it under stringent war conditions. This was the task that had to be accorded highest priority for the time being.

Given all this, Eugenia developed fresh responsibilities. It was down to her to take care of certain regions, particularly the north and west. One of her major foci was the concept of popular power: how to assess the rôle of a leadership within the nascent popular power movement and at the same time promote mass participation. One key concept central to Eugenia's militancy was her worry that there should be genuine mass participation from the base organisations in the coming revolution.

She always said that if, when power was gained, she was allowed to choose she would take one of two jobs: either working with the mass organisations, or in the building of the party. She used to call them two means of promoting public access to power. I would tease her by saying she'd end up either working for a government bureaucracy or off on international postings. She'd reply, fine, if I'm given one of those two jobs, I'd be true to my internationalist convictions and ask to go and fight in Guatemala.

Seven

I questioned the women commanders on the subject of children. Marta answered:

It's a serious problem. One can become incredibly involved in caring for them. It's essential to have great dedication in order to be capable of separating from one's child at any given moment.

Having children is the most beautiful experience there is, and the most revolutionary too, I believe. The state of war that's part of our strategy of prolonged popular warfare doesn't deprive you of the possibility of motherhood. Our organisation always nurtured family life, within the war situation and with all the limitations this imposes. What happens is that each phase in the war becomes even harsher.

For example, when I bore my first son, the conditions were different, although always very dangerous. One brings up the child accepting all the restrictions imposed by work, but within a proletarian and collectivist atmosphere. This helps one to complete projects, and to find it possible to be a parent at the same time. Up there in the interior it's now harder to have a baby at the front, but until 1980 the kids who lived with us led a normal family life.

It's a really lovely experience and also a great sacrifice. We mothers who are at the same time revolutionaries have still more sacrifices imposed upon us than the rest who aren't. We have to sleep less in order to work more.

For example, over Eugenia's daughter, it was the organisation's commitment to take and educate her as and when necessary. The organisation takes responsibility for those kids as far as it can. Only when there's no way out, when there's absolutely no one available, then the children get handed back to other relatives; but the party line is to keep them with us to form them according to the thinking of our organisation. If we hand them over to relatives, they could be raised according to different principles.

Nadia told me:

I married pretty young. Sometimes I think it was due to the early age at which I gave myself over to work that made me grow up prematurely. Any seventeen-year-old girl who goes on military operations, in the underground, develops a different psychological make-up.

The comrade I married is also a member of the organisation. I recruited him. We became involved within a few months of one another, and it's now three years since we parted on excellent terms. We're good friends, although there was a measure of misunderstanding on his side.

I'd get home late at night, sometimes I wouldn't make it at all, and perhaps because he knew I was engaged on revolutionary duties, perhaps due to his own formative years, he was a bit *macho*. I, for my part, was not all that able to get him to understand the exigencies imposed by my work. My husband came from a peasant background, it seemed to me from a very good home. We have a son who's now seven years old. The boy lived with us till he was a year old. Then it became impossible: it was impractical going into the countryside, attending meetings, etc. We couldn't accept employing someone to look after him, that's a contradiction.

At the end of that first year when he was a year old he went to live with my parents. I always visited him, until 1975 when my brother was killed in combat, along with his wife, and this generated a whole new family situation, given that all of us, in one way or another, were drawn into it.

For security reasons (the police constantly hounded me, knowing that my son was there with my parents and that I was bound to turn up at some time), fourteen months went by without my seeing him. It's the hardest trial I've been put through up until now.

He's still with my parents. When the surveillance was diminished, I re-established a level of communication with him, but of course it's neither daily nor even weekly. I've tried hard to concern myself with his emotional and political development; I've always talked this over with my parents. There's a perfect understanding between the child and ourselves, despite the fact that my husband and I are separated.

He sees both of us, he knows we're separated, he knows we love him. Now he's seven years old he begins to comprehend that his mum and dad are involved in important work on behalf of the poor. He understands according to his own lights, he knows he mustn't repeat what we say and it doesn't bother him. He's been put through some suffering, of course, as we too suffer.

We've managed to keep the channels open, a basic connection, an identity shared between him and ourselves, but we're obviously aware that under other circumstances the logical thing is for a child to be raised with his parents.

Under the war conditions and system imposed on our country, I don't feel my concern as a mother is restricted simply to one child, there are millions of children in the country. I even believe that I wouldn't have the moral qualifications to educate my son with, if I weren't directly taking part in my people's liberation. It's an act of hypocrisy to collaborate in the way things are in this country.

It's a contradiction, but one has to see how to resolve it. The interests of the whole population take first place, they're what have to prevail over all our personal activities. For me, the costs came high in learning this because of the pain it entailed, but I'm fully convinced that motherhood has a not merely personal but also an historical dimension.

'What can you tell us about children's participation in revolutionary tasks?' I asked Marta and Ondina.

'It's touching,' Marta answered. 'I've known many instances. Children start participating at around twelve years old when they're beginning to assume a sense of responsibility.'

'I knew a boy who was about seven,' Ondina said. 'He served as a courier. It was really moving, when he went along the street and maybe saw you, he wouldn't greet you, just looked away, and pretended he didn't know you.'

'In some districts, the children acted as look-out posts,' Marta said. "Here comes the patrol," they would say, "here comes the night watch." They acted, seeming to be playing in the street like the other children, and, if someone came by, they came inside to let us know.'

'As for us in the slums,' Ondina added, 'we set up kindergartens as a way of keeping the children with us. We taught them to read and write and so forth. This also served the purpose of instructing their parents too. The person who minds the children for a while in the morning, allows their mother to rest while the children learn. Sometimes there are no schools near enough to the slums, and so the children don't attend school. When one begins to deal with the children, to chat with them their mothers likewise grow in confidence. The child starts to identify, then comes along with us to paint slogans, join in demonstrations, etc. They help us to make banners, and they like doing it, and taking part.'

'If they happened to live in a liberated zone,' Marta said, 'they steeped themselves in the atmosphere and learned all our legends. They had a pretty sophisticated awareness of the enemy. I remember three orphans, we kept them with us, they were great. They were very perceptive, they gave the neighbours the line and everything. The littlest was only five. He would say "aunt" to whoever he was told to address in this way. The others were seven and nine.'

'Would you like to have children?' I asked Commander Ana Guadaloupe Martínez.

I believe that all of us women want to have children, and plenty of them [she answered]. I'll explain the schemes we sometimes discussed with our women comrades in respect of family life. It's curious that you don't think that a woman guerrilla wouldn't also think about having a family.

All of us, at least we women comrades within the leadership, have discussed how many children we want. Some of us said eight. At least to have one or two, but we'll go on to adopt at least another five. There are so many orphans. The idea is that they should all be the same age. Adopt a five-year-old, and then the rest, also aged five. Can you imagine it? It'd be an army in the home.

The number of orphans is really high. There's going to be a quantity of kids there who'll become our children. Our houses will be overflowing with children.

Eight

Mélida Anaya Montes deserves a chapter to herself. She is a tall, heavily-built woman with a severe hairstyle and rigid posture. Her expression, which is incisive when political matters are discussed, softens when she speaks of Eugenia, of Ana Patricia, or of any of the young men and women revolutionaries involved in the heroic stance taken by the Salvadorean people. She herself never married and regards them all as her own children.

Mélida is better known and admired by the Salvadorean people under her *nom de guerre*, Ana María, the legendary Ana María, second in command to the FPL's Commander Marcial, and member of the United Revolutionary Tendency (DRU) of the FMLN.

I was born on 17 May 1931 in a tiny village close to San Salvador [she recounted]. It's called Santiago de Texacuangos and lies 14 kilometres beyond San Salvador. It's a very pretty little place, graced with a panoramic view. You can see Ilopango perfectly, the hills of Cojutepeque and Las Pavas, and the airport. There's a particularly beautiful cottonwood tree, as common as it is everywhere in our country; but it's a lovely specimen in front of the church and beyond it the town hall.

Santiago de Texacuangos is a rugged little village with poor inhabitants. It's not noted for any special form of cultivation, though there are crops of beans, maize, and the occasional industry that established itself but which has died out. *Nahuilla* is made there, a sweet flavoured with brown loaf sugar. *Nahuilla* is still manufactured from time to time, but with nothing like the output of previous years. These things have declined in inverse ratio to the industrialisation taking place in the rest of the country.

Texacuangos is a hamlet well-known throughout the country. It has a special place in our folklore. Every July the feast of our patron saint is celebrated, and what's called our history is enacted. Two people dress up colourfully and dance, telling the story of the Spanish Conquest. Every year they perform this dance in front of the church and each of them relates a piece of our history. They are the historians.

Ana María studied in several of the country's cities. She obtained her teaching certificate in secondary education at the *Normal Superior*.[1] She graduated in Educational Sciences and worked as both a primary and secondary teacher. She was deputy head at the Spanish Teachers' Training College and head of studies in the *Normal Superior*.

When I worked at the *Normal Superior*, I took my first steps in the direction of trade unionism. I was the representative for a group of secondary teachers called the Association of Secondary Education Teachers. It was quite a small group. One fine day we met with comrade representatives from fellow organisations, and discussed forming a single association. On 14 September 1964, we got together and began work. We set up a coordinating committee for everything we wanted as demonstrated by our joint struggle. So the Teachers' Coordinating Committee was born, which had a large output of work, and a truly phenomenal success rate unequalled among teachers in El Salvador's history.

We held mass meetings and on one particular 21 June, the day before the national holiday for Teachers' Day, there were around 16,000 teachers congregated. The ensuing demonstration was only some 500 short of the 16,000. This was the fruit of all our labours.

I was on the leadership executive of the council. Later it joined what now goes by the name of the National Association of Salvadorean Educationalists (ANDES) of 21 June, in memory of this demonstration.

From the start, the salient characteristic of this association was its massive size. At the crux of the struggle, when teachers presented their proposals and their claims, the government as a last resort reverted to violence. Giant demonstrations were

---

[1] The most prestigious teachers' training college.

dispersed with tear-gas, etc. Since the participation was on a mass scale, so was the rise in consciousness.

I remember that back in '68 there was a teachers' strike, without precedent in the country's history. We occupied the Education Ministry, and remained there for two months. Two months that weren't spent sitting on our behinds. Thousands and thousands of people assembled in the square outside; almost the entire population of San Salvador came by. This contributed to the fact that alongside the study we personally undertook and alongside its practice, one learned more and more clearly that the peaceful way forward was closed to us in El Salvador. The solidarity offered us by the workers during the strike, the assassination of two of our comrades, the whole configuration of events put me through a process of growing up that went way beyond the limits of the strike.

In 1971 I was in direct contact with Commander Salvador Cayetano Carpio. In 1970 there already existed the seeds of what has since become the FPL. I moved in those circles. At that time they were tiny, very close-knit, the movement was beginning, and already acquiring its dimension of struggle. From then on, I dedicated myself wholeheartedly to the revolutionary struggle.

I entered the organisation secretly, but I didn't immediately go underground. I was in the open struggle but already with some sense of my bearings. That's how the teaching profession came to exercise a direct influence on the advance positions being established in El Salvador.

I completed my official term as secretary-general of ANDES and from 1973 on I went underground. From then on I was fully committed to the FPL, in the greatest secrecy. It's an integral part of my life.

'How did you get to know Eugenia?' I asked.

I began working with Eugenia when she was selected as a member of the organisational committee. It was there I came to know her personally. Within the secret cells we only know each other under code-names, one can know someone's work well in every detail without being able to recognise any of the workers by sight.

It was in that way I knew of Eugenia's work. It was later on I knew her personally, when the organisation's work became my charge. Eugenia's contribution had been a very positive one, her work with the peasants being one of the FPL's cornerstones. She

112

was one of the main recruiters and organisers within FECCAS, and worked very hard in that organisation too. We knew of her sensitivity, her original perceptions and her capacity for work.

When she moved on to the organisational committee, I was put in direct charge of her and was in a position to appreciate her personal qualities. The first of these was her Marxist-Leninist perception of the world, her formation as a militant to be taken seriously within the framework of the organisation.

My own inclination is to take a look at someone's personal qualities, their human side. These have something permanent to teach, much more so than intellectual formulations. Of course, the latter is important and has to be taken into account, but it lacks value without the human qualities.

Looking at the practical side of things, I had received news of her capacity for work and organisaton, her far-sightedness and self-discipline. On my arrival, it was this practical side of her that immediately struck me. She decided on the security precautions for the house, and set in motion everything the organisation had taught from the beginning. This too attracted my attention.

Eugenia had a treasure of a little girl and for me this was one of those things that touched my heart. I know from my own experience how hard a revolutionary's life is. The revolutionary has to abandon her family. Of course, she's fighting for the supreme values, but in practice these have to be suppressed for short periods. It has to be so. Eugenia was a woman with very little time. She introduced the child into the collective.

I was very moved on my first day, when she took the little girl into her arms and told her: 'I've got to go away, you stay here with your mummy, because she *is* your mummy. And here's your aunt,' she indicated someone else, 'she'll see to changing your nappies. You can settle down quietly with your mummy and your aunts.'

She was integrating her emotionally, detaching herself from her. It's possible for a mother's natural and rightful egotism to be irreproachable but she, in her knowledge of the revolutionary's life, emotionally integrated her daughter into the collective.

Eugenia paid a lot of attention to her comrades. I witnessed her management of the collective on several occasions, I could see her concern that the comrades all got fed, her worry over the security of the house, over the little girl, over everything. Perhaps what was most outstanding in her was her synthesis as a revolutionary, mother, comrade and wife. It's not easy to live out such an integrated perspective in practice. Eugenia confronted death without wavering.

Javier continued:

Already in what one can see of the child's development, I think there are signs that show her to be Eugenia's daughter. She had a certain number of clearly thought-out attitudes she wanted to imprint on our daughter: for example a lack of dependence upon her mother and father. This made us take certain decisions – for example that she should sleep alone, that she adapt to sleeping with different adults in the house – and these left their mark in making the child content to stay with anyone. For Eugenia, there was a particular charm in her daughter's relationship with the other comrades.

Eugenia was always an extraordinarily tender woman in her relationship with me, illustrated by details like this: I'm very fond of peanuts, they're frequently unobtainable but whenever I got home I always found little bags of them on my pillow. It meant that she had stopped off at the house. Sometimes she would attempt to restrain the expression of such tenderness, when we were in the company of other comrades. However, I always told her that I couldn't reproach her for her attitude to the little girl. There she would always go over the top. This sweetness contrasted with her discipline, the firmness she always displayed in her revolutionary work. But the child was never turned into an obstacle to her revolutionary commitments, nor were these allowed to hinder our daughter's education. She always resolved the contradiction, such a hard one in the life of a revolutionary, and one which so often causes serious conflict.

For the first six months of her life, Ana Patricia lived with her mother. For reasons to do with his task, Javier had to live elsewhere and visit them when it was possible. In June 1980 a major security scare arose in the house where Eugenia and her child were living. Javier described Eugenia's response to this emergency:

It became necessary to evacuate the house at once and I wasn't around. It was out of the question to take the child along when transporting all the arms and possessions. All the comrades had to take refuge in other houses and they all wondered what Eugenia would do with her child.

Without vacillating, she caught up Ana Patricia and took her to a woman comrade's house. She told her: 'Look, I don't know how we're going to sort this one out, but I know that you'll look after her,' and – bang – handed her over. She then returned to all her chores. Despite the great love she felt for her daughter, she knew how to detach herself when she had to do so for the sake of her work and the struggle.

When Javier learned what had happened, he went to collect Ana Patricia. He had to look after her for the next six weeks. When the security threat abated, Ana Patricia returned to her mother, and Javier had to leave them both in order to finish a project that had been assigned to him. He was reunited with them in August 1980, and from then on the three of them lived together until preparations began for the general offensive of January 1981. Recalling those months, Javier said:

I think that if any woman comrade ever lived fully with her child, that comrade was Eugenia. Without forfeiting her total commitment to the revolution (or *because* of it, as she saw things), she gave herself utterly to her child's education. She implanted a series of behaviour patterns that can now be clearly seen. The girl has learned that if someone gives her sweets, then she immediately shares them out with the assembled company.

Another anecdote which illuminates Eugenia's temperament runs as follows. On one occasion the girl fell ill and we didn't know what was wrong, she wouldn't stop crying, and had a temperature. It was two in the morning. It's very dangerous to go out in search of a doctor in San Salvador at such an hour. Eugenia never lost her composure. She went and ferreted out a book to look up and discover how we could assess what was happening to the little girl. She figured out what was wrong and was in the event proved correct.

'Describe an average day in Eugenia's life during this period,' I suggested.

She was already on the national committee of the Central Command when we were living together [he said]. She was given the task of visiting the regions. She was fanatically tidy. However many jobs she had on, she always took the time before leaving to sweep up, make the bed, getting me to do my share; then seeing to the little girl and getting her ready, giving her a wash and then the bottle, etc.

She'd go out, take the bus for the western zone where she'd probably have to visit some remote corner, or to an area where she needed to meet with the local organiser, or a municipal leader. She'd leave the house at six-thirty or seven o'clock. She often travelled with politically sensitive papers and had to go armed.

One time, returning from one of her visits to Santa Ana, the bus she was travelling on was halted. She had a whole lot of papers in her bag. A police road-block of some thirty guards held them up. They stopped the bus and wouldn't let the people out as they had on other occasions. They began to search through the rows of seats, two guards working from the front and two from the back. She was beside the window, next to a young lad. Across the way, a little old lady was seated. While Eugenia was watching the guards advancing, what happened was that she began to think of her daughter, of me. She marked out mentally where she'd have to fire, who she'd have to shoot in order to break out. She opened the zip on her bag and waited.

She had incredible luck: the guards searching from the front to the back stopped one row ahead of where she was sitting, and those working from the back broke off at the row behind her. The only row they didn't search was hers.

Eugenia usually returned the same day, perhaps the next day, always with her tasks completed. She had the necessary meetings with her cell and saw all the people she had to see in San Salvador. The work took from six a.m. until eleven, midnight or one the next morning. She'd return home at eight-thirty or nine, but resume working. There were always men or women comrades to take care of the girl. Despite this routine, Eugenia sought out ways of finding time to pay attention to her daughter and to share with me – maintaining the necessary compart-mentalisation of her work, her worries, and Ana Patricia's education.

Nine

Marina González is a typical Salvadorean proletarian woman, a Mother Courage from Cuscatlán, whose biography is included here because it could well be representative of thousands upon thousands of lives denied, lives at once anonymous and combative.

Marina never knew Eugenia personally but, like a great many other women committed to the Salvadorean struggle, she knew of her revolutionary reputation and unreservedly admired her. It's more than likely that the two of them crossed in the mass demonstrations of 1976 before Eugenia went underground, given that Marina was a BPR organiser for that year.

If President Reagan and his advisors really want to know why the Salvadorean people are up in arms, they'd understand a lot more from Marina González's biography than from searching for proof of hypothetical conspiracies of Cuban or Russian origin.

Marina was one of 11 children. She lived with all her family in one room on a farm. There were three beds: up to four children slept together in a single one. Her father was a tailor and his earnings were inadequate to feed the family.

What's more [Marina said], the society that surrounded also corrupted us. My father was an alcoholic, he'd spend six months on end drinking. My mother had to go out to do washing and ironing. The poor woman sometimes rose at three in the morning, and sundown found her still at the ironing board, in order simply to provide us with a notebook or a pencil.

We reached the sixth grade, barefoot. Mealtimes in the morning consisted of a cup of coffee and a roll. We went to school without a penny in our pockets. I remember that when I saw other kids peeling mangoes, I begged for the skins. I remember dropping out of school for six months at a time, because they told us to bring in books or material for class activities, or money for school repairs. I didn't have any money and it seemed better to give up attending. That way I lost three years' schooling. I got through my primary grades at evening class.

From the age of 13, I started work in a sweet factory. I wrapped the sweets and earned a *peso* a day. I worked there all day, then went on to evening classes. The boss there was thoroughly rude. When I got hungry I ate some crisps, as they had a shop selling crisps and sweets. But the boss told me to go to hell. His wife came from a poor background and she called me over, but the man told me to leave the food alone, as he'd already paid me. 'Get on with your work,' he ordered me, 'but I don't want you to keep stuffing yourself with my crisps.'

I moved on to the 'Suez' shirt-makers. I worked as a cleaner in the store. When I'd finished the cleaning, I brought in the bread, then the milk, and then they sent me over to the shirt factory. They paid me two *pesos* a day. I arrived at seven in the morning and got out at six in the evening. At lunch break I had to go and wash the dishes and clean the house in order to earn something to eat. At home I was never able to obtain even a scrap of meat.

Then I joined the 'Maidenform' factory. There were about 30 sewing-machines together with those they started out with, and four work-benches. There I earned two and a half *pesos* or a dollar a day, and worked for eight hours. As the factory was only getting under way and I wanted to learn more, in practice I worked nearer nine or ten hours. We had to be trained to make a bra called 'She'. They brought the fabric and everything in from the United States. They re-exported the finished products, had them packaged, then they came back into El Salvador again to be sold.

The Maidenform company is one of many multinationals that put down roots in El Salvador during the 1960s. As one gathers from Marina's story, the company imported the cloth, elastic and metal parts from the US, sending the completed garment back to the United States to be packaged. All that remained in El Salvador were the starvation wages paid out to Marina and her work-mates. A North American employee would have earned at least $35 a day for the work

Marina was paid one dollar to do. A simple calculation shows that the company saved $320,000 a year just by exploiting Marina and her twenty-nine Salvadorean work-mates as a source of cheap labour. The factory expanded, predictably enough, and had to move to the Boulevard del Ejército. Marina continued:

They were even making soldiers' kits to be sent out to Vietnam. These were large, olive-green knapsacks. They sent some special machines over for this and needed to take on extra staff. Those who'd learned most about making bras were transferred to the soldiers' kits. I was assigned to putting the clips on to the elastic. They sent over everything we needed. At first they paid me two and a half *pesos* a day, and later on three *pesos* and 20 cents. This was the highest rate I received. Once the war in Vietnam was over, no more knapsacks were produced. Then, to maintain their level of exploitation, they put us on to making girdles. Eventually we were making roll-ons and the whole Maidenform range of goods.

The supervisor had promised me that soon I'd be earning plenty of money, so I carried on working in the hope of it until I realized that five years had gone by with me still stuck on the same wage. The assistant manager was one Julio Salinas and I told him 'I've got to earn more than this.' I already had three kids and couldn't make ends meet. He agreed with me, and said he'd go and speak to Señor Torbú.

The way it went was that they advised me I'd have to produce eight or nine garments a day, and could make up to twenty if I wished. When they said eight or nine, that cheered me up and I said okay, fine. I began with eight. A week went by and I still had the same wage packet. I returned for another talk with Señor Salinas. He went to the manager and reported back: 'He says you have to make ten garments.' That's also when I learned how they'd be getting me to turn out twenty and again I'd get the same weekly wage. That's when I became annoyed.

The management viewed Marina as a 'subversive' for not being satisfied with her wages. They threatened to suspend any employee found talking with her. There were also other threats doled out by the management.

If anyone was five minutes late, if someone turned up at five past eight, they got a black mark, and they had to stay behind and work an extra half hour in order not to lose the day's wage. So they stopped behind and made a present to the factory of the additional 25 minutes. Late, they'd say, blowing the whistle and bolting the door. As I lived far away, I had to leave everything ready prepared for the kids and so forth, and I might arrive late and remain outside. Then I'd go back home, because earning one *peso* 60 cents for a half-day's work wasn't worth it, I couldn't even buy the food with that. However cheap it might be, it couldn't cost less than 75 cents. Three days the same thing happened and, as there were no unions or anything, and I now had three black marks ... even the Employment Ministry had established that if they were clocked up within the month, you could be sacked without any form of compensation whatever.

That was the reason they gave for wanting to throw me out, but they couldn't because I was about to have my fourth baby. Taking stock of my problems, that no one would talk to me, that I was somewhat like the ugly duckling because I wouldn't allow myself to be exploited as they wanted, I began to think. I wanted to earn more, and I'd got it into my head that no way was I going to produce as much as before.

I had a seven-year-old girl and the next arrived requiring my care. I went to the Employment Ministry to see if they could do anything to help; they didn't offer a thing. They advised me to return and get stuck back into my work. I could see I wasn't wanted and abandoned my seven wasted years.

Marina's husband also experienced the pitiless exploitation to which the Salvadorean working-class is exposed. Marina explained:

When I had my first baby, I moved out from my parents' place. We lived in a tiny house over in Soyapango, a two-roomed effort. In one room lived my mother-in-law and in the other ourselves. But it so happened that my husband was also a worker and worked in another *gringo* factory, an aluminium one at Alcoa.

My husband earned five *colones* a day. It was customary to pay men more. They produced things like Venetian blinds and tubes at Alcoa – but one has to take into account that in earning those five *colones* they were still super-exploited. They had to smelt the aluminium and the heat was cruel, it was dehydrating.

Although they were better paid, it didn't have a lot to do with what they should have earned.

Nevertheless, we were still obliged to go and live elsewhere. We couldn't pay for anywhere, so we got a small plot outside the area, in the Plan del Pino. We had to fall back on the idea of a smallholding and start building a shack, a sort of barn made only of mud and corrugated iron, coated inside with cardboard and dried shrubbery. That's how we started, and we continued adding the bits of brushwood, lashed with rope. My husband would have to go out at four in the afternoon to make the mud-daub out of earth and water and use it for plastering the walls. So we arrived at making our little house; it's anyone's guess if it's still there.

From this little hovel we had to go on foot over some fields and along some paths to Soyapango to catch the bus, the number 13 to the factory. This meant we had to leave home at six a.m. to be at work by eight o'clock.

After Marina left her job in the Maidenform factory to look after her four children, her husband joined up as an activist, organising a union in the Alcoa factory to fight for better pay and conditions. The new unionists came out on strike and the National Guard locked them out of the factory.

As my husband had left at eight in the morning and still wasn't back at five in the afternoon I went out to see what was going on. I found him at the CUSS [United Confederation of Salvadorean Trade Unionists] office. As we went on back, I told him that as a union rep he had to struggle to reach his goal; even if he had to do so on behalf of the other comrades, that he should never for an instant abandon the cause of the worker, because trust had been placed in him as a union leader, and he had to fight every inch of the way with them.

With her husband out on strike, it fell to Marina to support the family. How could she do this with four small children?

We'd been lent 300 *colones*,' she explained, 'and we rented a freezer. I made and kept ice lollies in this freezer. I bought the fruit and made them myself. Then I went and sold them outside

121

certain schools, and also supplied them to shops at around 20 per cent. I told my husband to carry forward the struggle and he told me right, that was fine then. So he was sacked from his job and paid off with a mere 1,500 *pesos* for eleven years' work. They never gave them what each worker actually merited. They threw out every single person who had anything to do with the union, and the factory was left to tick over with a few old men hand-picked by the management.

Her husband had been put out of work not only in Alcoa but everywhere else too. He soon found out that the Salvadorean bosses had blacklisted him for the crime of being a well-known unionist.

From then on my husband was out of work. As a unionist, it was hopeless attempting to find work anywhere. On top of this, they were always looking for younger types with a higher level of output. He was in despair and looked to a friend with a sister in Canada.

We had almost finished paying for our little plot. We handed over fifteen *colones* monthly. We had to mortgage our shack for his trip to Canada. He was going to work in a factory over there but as he entered as a tourist, by the back door, they deported him. He only got to stay there a year and a half. Since he's been back from there, he's still not worked, as things in El Salvador have taken a new twist.

He got back in '78. The situation had become more difficult. He brought some money with him and bought a pick-up truck, but it didn't do him any good since he just can't get work in El Salvador. The only possibility left open to us was to involve ourselves in the struggle for the people's rights.

'When did you begin to think in political terms?' I asked her.

I started from the basis of my own experience, with the same exploitation forever being handed out. One works and works and never gets ahead. There's no way out of the rut.

I sent my kids to school. I told them all that I'd been put through, and they suffered it to a lesser degree. That's how one gains in consciousness of how to organise. It's the only way in which to make the people's interests prevail.

Some Christian communities were getting off the ground and

invited me in. I began to see what was really taking place on a national scale and everything they told me about there was peanuts compared to my own experience. But the Christian communities explained how it all came about.

I was with some Spanish nuns. I began to hear whisperings about demonstrations. At the same time as religion can draw you on, at other times it can hold you back. They tell you not to kill and I don't know what else, but if a crowd of police descend, what's one supposed to do? I liked the option picked out by the nun who told me that you had to defend yourself. Fine, we're in business together, I told her.

By then Rutilio Grande had been killed and during the funeral I could see how the people were on the point of revolt, chanting: 'Who killed you?' 'The fascist military tyranny.' 'Who will avenge you?' 'The people will.'

I felt those slogans echo within me. I longed to be a part of that organised sector of the people. Father Colorado was a priest who wouldn't get off the fence, was neither fish nor fowl. But the tyranny regarded him as a communist, even though that was nothing to do with him. He preached the gospels and that was the sum of it. He withdrew and stopped coming to say Mass to us. He was afraid, and buried himself in the mountains.

So they sent us Ernesto Barrera. And when he preached I felt my hopes being fulfilled. I went and said to him, 'Father, I wish to confess.' I managed to tell him all the doubts on my conscience. The elections between Romero and Claramount were about to take place. I saw that neither offered us a way forward.

'Look here, Father,' I told him, 'I've seen everything going on among the people, and I want to know in which ways I can help their interests to prevail.'

He asked me some questions. 'Are you from ANDES?' he said. 'Where from, then?' he added. I told him from nowhere in particular. The only thing plain to me was that the people needed another way to unfold and develop. He asked me if there were other comrades who shared my concern, and I answered yes.

'Good,' he said. 'One day soon we'll hold a meeting.'

It was Palm Sunday, the day when Jesus entered Jerusalem on a donkey. We discussed matters and decided to wait for Ascension Day. I already knew Valentín (who was to die with Fr Barrera), and we began a little group. We analysed our lives, and

123

that was how our consciousness began to be raised.

I joined the organisation in 1976, and my husband signed up as soon as he came back from Canada. He returned to me an alienated man, having become used to living in a well-appointed flat, and he felt frustrated when he returned to that patch of hick country where we lived without electricity or water, and with quagmires whenever it rained.

So I said to him: 'Well, we've both come back home worse off than we started out. Instead of recognising how capitalism tries to keep other nations subjected to misery, you turn up here moaning. You have to be realistic.'

Because he came to me with such a sense of alienation, he wanted me to concern myself more with domestic matters, but it was already too late for him to restrict me like this.

Marina's conversations with her husband took effect. When he discovered that running his truck wasted more in petrol than he managed to earn, and since he couldn't obtain employment because he was still on the bosses' blacklist, he too decided to join the organised working class and dedicate himself to working for the revolution full-time. As always, it fell to Marina to support the family.

Our organisation never gave us any help in coping with our finances; everyone had to fend for themselves economically. The leadership never told us 'You'll have a home, you'll be taken care of,' because everyone who enlisted had to do so without seeking personal gain. Every moment was spent in consideration of the good of the greatest number. That's why I could never really enrol full-time. I couldn't undertake work with the masses. The enemy had by then located me and I was a marked woman. I had to move on to other assignments, but it so happened that as my husband had already become involved it wasn't practicable for the two of us to work; someone had to take care of the house and keep things going. He certainly put in his twenty-four hours a day, and the truck was used for his new activities. That's how we always managed to maintain a high level of activity.

Throughout 1979 I sold ice-lollies at the school, but during the holidays we had no source of income. So it occurred to me to sell fruit in the Soyapango market. At the end of 1979 there followed another period when I was out of work, which I confided to a woman who supplied the Soyapango market with cakes and pastries. 'Niña Vilma,' I told her, 'I can't find work at all.'

She'd been supplied with a load of little toys from Hong Kong. So she asked me, 'Well, why don't you have a go at selling these?' She gave me an advance, I seized a large basketful, and off I went.

For this I earned 25 *centavos* a small box. It didn't seem to me they were selling well. So I suggested to Doña Vilma that it might be better for me to pay her later, when the toy season was at its height and invert the usual procedure. She agreed. So I brought in balls and other toys, mostly from my own stock, and we sold them in the street. That's how I made out.

Marina had taken part in the occupation of the Employment Ministry and of the 'El León' and 'Diana' factories. She worked in with the employees at the Gloria, National, International and IMES industries. Her organisation selected her to be in charge of information on the Trades Union Coordinating Committee, but she found herself unable to accept because of continuing family commitments.

I asked her why she had to flee El Salvador and take refuge in Nicaragua.

I left our home in 1980 because the enemy was searching and destroying the Christian communities in our area. A nun let me know: 'Marina, there's a death squad in front of your house, pointing it out and directing other people towards it.' She was a Spanish nun from the Basque region and really on the ball. She supported us in every way.

We lived in a real hole. It was an impossible house to make secure, made of mud and corrugated iron, falling apart at the seams. I looked out of the top and saw two strange men. They were saying, 'See, she's not coming', and in the end they went off.

I had to start looking out for myself, and it was obvious I had to quit the house. I moved into another lent me by my nephew. The house wasn't finished, it didn't have electricity or anything, but there was no other way out. I took my children and husband. The tyranny didn't bother finding out if I was the activist; they were happy to hit the whole family. We'd already seen how in several places corpses had started appearing, sometimes mutilated. They'd reached the stage of doing away with whole families. Their bodies were found hanging, with their heads torn off or their hands or their feet. To begin with they chucked the corpses down ravines; more recently they took pleasure in putting them on display, leaving them out on the motorways so that people would see them and feel intimidated.

My brother, also recruited into the organisation, sent me a hundred *pesos*. That started me off again in search of means to support my kids. I collected the freezer, and left the rest of our stuff. I made a bit of a shop there in our home, but in July last year I had to get out once more.

I later figured out that a woman comrade I'd recruited had been taken prisoner. They said it was a miracle that she'd been left alive. This woman didn't know where I lived, she only knew I had this little shop, and roughly whereabouts it was. In addition, my brother-in-law had been told that one of the soldiers had a tape-recorder and a recording of my voice. I can well believe it, since in the school where we held our meetings even the walls had ears, literally!

I didn't pay too much heed to any of this, and then my mother and sister arrived and told me: 'Marina, get out of here.'

My husband wasn't around as he was busy elsewhere, there were only the children and myself. My mum took the kids. My mother and sister began crying. So I told her: 'Mother, don't cry. If years ago you'd struggled for our people's freedom, we'd all now be in very different circumstances.'

For some time my thoughts had been turning in the direction of the armed struggle, but who could I leave the children with? My mother wouldn't take the responsibility for them, nor would my sister.

'Look, Mum,' my sister had warned her, 'it'll be her turn next to get bumped off and it'll be her own fault. It would have been better if we'd taken charge of the kids.' They hugged me and said goodbye as if they'd never see me again, because I didn't want to step outside the house.

I shut all the doors to the house and was on my own. I remember myself then without a thing in the world but my high spirits. The only thing I'll do, I told myself, is shout revolutionary slogans. That was how I spent the next two nights. On the Sunday my husband arrived and was astonished at not finding the children. I explained it all to him and we went round to my mum's. The boy came to Nicaragua with us and the girls followed. And now I sell *pupusas*[1] in Estelí.

126

Marina paused and reflected on her long *via crucis*. She added: 'I saw how, at the beginning, the people in the regions were afraid of our organisation. Later on the work developed and so it progressed. The work kept moving on even when one was taking risks.

'Here I feel myself to be out of reach of the enemy, but one longs to be in the midst of our own people. The Nicaraguan revolution is also a part of our experience, we share the same enemy. If there is outside intervention, we must also give our support. Every people engaged in struggle has to believe that it's everyone's struggle.

'I'm in struggle,' Marina concluded, 'so that my children won't have to be, or if they do it'll be in defence of what we've handed on to them.'

---

[1] Stuffed maize pancakes sold on griddles in the street – the national dish of El Salvador.

Ten

The Unified Revolutionary Tendency (DRU) of the FMLN decided to launch a general offensive on 10 January 1981. Among the decisive reasons for selecting that date was the fact that the reactionary Ronald Reagan was to assume the US presidency on 20 January, and had made clear his intention of supporting the Salvadorean junta with all the economic and military aid necessary to smash the country's revolutionary movement.

December 1980 was a month of major preparations within all the politico-military organisations forming the FMLN. Eugenia, who was working in the organising committee of the northern zone, was transferred to the San Salvador metropolitan zone.

The FPL's Felipe Peña front included the capital's northern sector and the regions of Cuscatlán, Libertad and parts of Cabañas.

'I led the front for that area,' Commander Ricardo recalled. 'When I learned that they were sending Eugenia to the metropolitan zone, I immediately sought to persuade her to involve herself in the General Staff.'

It was the first time that Eugenia formally enlisted in the military ranks, but this didn't cause Ricardo any concern. 'She'd already had considerable experience of small military actions,' he said, 'especially within the "armed propaganda" campaign. She had also received a basic military training.'

Ricardo had a serious problem with the logistics of his security infrastructure and in supplying and feeding his military units. It seemed to him that Eugenia, with her clear outlook and her proven organisational capacity, offered the solution he was looking for. He told me: 'There were some comrades there without organisational understanding. It was partly due to them that Eugenia entered the General Staff and was handed responsibility for the whole department we call the Service Section.'

As the person in charge of that section, Eugenia had to resolve the problem of supplying food, medicine and clothing. Besides this, she had to organise logistic networks, setting up a structure to make arrangements for hygiene to fit the exigencies of the general offensive and, finally, to assume within her responsibility all the small-arms workshops operating in her zone.

'We only managed to work together in December 1980,' continued Ricardo. 'She succeeded in coordinating the whole area very well. She accomplished an extraordinary level of work during that month. She worked day and night. She was like a little ant. When I called to let her know what was going on there, she told me: "Look, I don't know anything about all this. I don't know if I'll get it right for you."

' "You'll learn on your feet," I told her, "I have to have everything ready for 4 January."

'She set up all the security bases we needed in order for us to prepare the offensive.'

The organisation had entrusted Javier with certain undertakings outside the country, and Eugenia and Ana Patricia were sharing a safe house with some other comrades. In the midst of her myriad activities, Eugenia didn't neglect her daughter's education. Ricardo provided an anecdote which illuminated this period.

It was already the last few days in December. In all the rush of the preparations, we were busy drawing up plans and Ana Patricia began to make a nuisance of herself in order to attract her mother's attention. Eugenia told her to leave the room. Ana Patricia paid no heed to such an extent that her mother had to scold her and at that point she left in tears.

The minute the meeting finished, Eugenia went in search of the child and cuddled her. She continued integrating the little girl from her earliest beginnings, not only, let us say, into a mother's love but also initiating her moral upbringing from then on in. It followed that the child, although without full political understanding, was fully participating in the revolutionary process from the moment she went to live in one of the organisation's safe houses. Eugenia was amply confident that putting her child into the care of the organisation was tantamount to caring for her herself.

Marta recounted:

I said goodbye to Eugenia on 17 December. We were in the midst of preparing for the offensive and I knew she had to be got out. We said goodbye then because the atmosphere was already one of insurrection. We were working together in the same cell throughout the months of November and December. We'd never worked together, we'd always been in separate cells before. This time we shared our assignments and we were working comrades for the first time.

We said goodbye and she told me: 'Fine, let's see if we can stay alive.' She was excited about going to the front. I was also supposedly going to a front, but in effect got sent on an assignment abroad. On the 17th I said to her: 'I'll be back on the 19th, let's see if we can meet.'

We were then in a car-park in the Metro Centro, discussing our children and where we were going to leave them. I have two, a boy and a girl. Her attitude was one of 'Fine, for the moment we have to drop everything, but there's a great joy for us in going to the front.' That was the last time I saw her.

I saw her for the last time in a restaurant [Ondina recalled]. They also gave me an assignment abroad. We met to bid our farewells, because she already knew I was going to leave the country.

It'd been a long time since I'd seen her. I'd just miscarried, so she came over to see how I was and all the rest of it, but I never thought it'd be for the last time. We made use of the opportunity to chat about the family, about my mum and my brothers. She was in closer touch with our family over this period. She went on to tell me that the task I'd been assigned was an important one. That always counted for a lot. It's a big shock to be told you're leaving the country. I was somewhat disappointed to be going abroad, but she told me not to be, that the project was worthwhile. She said that everything done for the people is important and that it would help the agricultural workers to advance; one had to do everything possible to develop work abroad, as much as in the interior.

'What are your strongest memories of Eugenia?' I asked Ondina.

She sang really out of tune. I'd go out in the car with her and she'd always be singing. She was an absent-minded driver. She finished off all the cars belonging to the house. Once she almost wrote off a Toyota engine because she went through a pothole. I missed seeing it. She always had her favourite songs she sang as she went along. There was one with the refrain, 'We shall not be moved.' Every time I hear it I think of her. Each time we went out she'd say: 'Let's sing, let's sing.'

She was really happy. We made a joke of it. She was happy to be doing the chores, but we rejected the milieu in which we were born; it was an uncomfortable one for us, and we'd had no access to other sources of amusement. What we then came to have were meetings, a different form of activity.

Eugenia was pretty sentimental. She couldn't fight with my mother or anything because she'd already be in tears and tears prevented her from speaking. She always did everything at full speed; she even ate at full speed. She was super-active, from five in the morning until eight at night, always on the run. I used to beg her: 'Hang on a second, let's talk,' and she'd answer, 'I'm coming, I'm coming. Oh, I've forgotten something.'

At the end of December, Eugenia wrote the following letter to Javier:

My Darling Love,

Before I begin, a huge kiss and hug from the little fatty and me. Words fail to say how much we miss you and how this separation hurts us.

Everything here at our venture is speeding up. I've now been told I'm off to work with Uncle Alex,[1] and they've assured me of a metropolitan branch. You can imagine how big a responsibility this is, but it's vital to our venture.

I hope to give it my all, it's going to be difficult and complicated, it's necessary to shoulder it all and throw oneself into the final effort, but most important of all the rewards to our undertaking will be beyond measure.

The girl isn't too well, she hasn't managed to settle. Her nasal

---

[1] The leader responsible for her work and development

catarrh has persisted all week, along with her sore throat and diarrhoea. I've taken her along to the doctor twice since you spoke to him, but she's suffered a high temperature and even though it's dropped a lot, she's got almost no appetite, something unusual for her. She's very pale which worries me, though today there's less opportunity to be worried as they've assigned me my sister's job in Peñón, so I'll have to be off and see her less.

How I want to share it all with you. The tension is so high I've lost all my appetite and I've got butterflies in my stomach, but as I know I've got to be in top condition, I'll take vitamins. Aside from that I'm fine, finishing off things as we'll be leaving this department which will close down in January. If all goes well, we'll meet on the 4th.

I think, I feel – it seems to me an objective fact – that your departure has affected her. When she hears a car she points at the door with her finger and calls: 'Daddy, Daddy, Daddy.' Suddenly she's started saying 'Daddy'. When she sees men she stares at them. One day when she saw Justo she took to stroking his arm and gave him a kiss (just as she does with you).

She misses your spoiling her and your cuddles, your caresses. I feel she's become less demonstrative.

I arrived when it was late. It's now urgent she leaves even though it hurts me. I saw your superior yesterday and he gave me your letters, my love. I love you, I could hardly bring myself to speak to him, but he chatted to me about the tape recorder and about our daughter. I hope I can talk to you on the 27th, but if not Beatriz' mum will and you can explain things to her. I need to know what things our little girl needs aside from her birth certificate which I hope they'll finally give me today. If not, the best thing is for me to speak to you on Monday, around two-thirty, so we can organise things for Monday 29th, if not we'll speak to you on Saturday after you've seen your superior. So, it's fixed for Monday 29th (we can talk openly, can't we?). It'll have to be quick, as my sister will be going on to your superior and I'll have to leave. My love, whatever happens I'll arrange everything to do with the journey to her granny as soon as I have the birth certificate. It's urgent, because everything's on the boil down here.

My love, we're in the final stage, and we have to give it our all, I'm prepared and confident, I know it's hard and I have to show my mettle in this operations centre. I want to tell you that I love you for ever, each day I love you more and each day your absence cuts me more deeply. I'll do my best to take care of myself, for the little one's sake, and soon we can fall into each other's arms. Hopefully that can be on the fourth.

It's six in the morning, I've got to leave. Dear one, this letter can't express the half of what I want to say to you, or to tell you how I miss you, but I feel you so close at times like this. I can't continue, I've got to go, later I'll write at greater leisure.

My love, *all* my strength, energy, everything goes out to you. A giant kiss from our little girl and an endless cuddle from the two of us. I'll bring you the photos on the fourth, and if not I'll send them later. I'm sending you the tape recorder without extension lead, since Ruth took it with her, do you remember?

Lots of kisses, I love you always, I miss you.

This letter was returned to Eugenia and she included it with a second one, dated 26 December 1980.

It's 10.05 at night
26 Dec: 3yrs 10 mths

My Darling Love,

It's the 26th, I remember you so closely, everything progressing in the middle of difficulties and problems. At an internal level, the decisions taken within the cell have gone slowly and are shifting. I'm stopping with Uncle Alex, at first I was told to remain in the centre, but today my sister told me that I've been ordered to go to Naranja at the earliest opportunity; I think that this is definite.

You sent a letter with Esteban, a reply to my two previous ones, but he or Ana never reached the contacts. The hardest part is that today my letter has been handed back to me. Last night I received the letter you sent me with Pavel. I didn't know there was a chance of seeing you on the 18th, so I haven't prepared the ground. Seeing you on the 4th will be difficult if I have to leave for Naranja this week, at least this seems to be the case. Today's Friday and I'll see Diana tomorrow. We have our final cell meeting this Sunday, which makes it impossible for me to come on the 28th.

I'm considering two alternatives: sending the little poppet to you with Pavel or have Mum bring her to you on the 28th.

You'll have to tell me if you agree about my mum. I can speak to you on that Saturday at six-thirty in the evening to clarify what we're doing.

As there were problems in the region where Uncle Al's the

boss they all nearly got killed, but in fact only one died, and the person with former responsibility for Naranja broke his foot and is incapacitated, which makes me think I'll be going there, and ought to be there now as the work is lagging badly behind, which makes it difficult for me to see you on the 4th.

My love, as regards our correspondence, I think it's going to be very hard going, especially for yours to me (at least by writing). I think you have to let me know if I can speak to you by phone at a particular date and time, at least to leave you a message. I could speak to you when I have a spare moment, or else I could leave it as read according to how I feel. I'll try to speak to you on Monday 29th.

My head's in a turmoil, but I'm well and I remember and feel you constantly with me, my love. There's no doubt but that I'll love you for ever and that my love for you grows without end. I love you, my love, and long for the day when the three of us can be together.

Just thinking about our little poppet leaving tugs at my heart and I know how it'll hurt me to be apart from the two of you. I know I don't have to tell you all this, since it's what you're experiencing being away from us both. It seems that on the 28th we'll finish here and everyone'll go to take up their new posts.

At the moment there's a real mess within the cell, we're dreadfully behind, but in other ways things are progressing.

I can also hear a major shoot-out, can't yet tell where, but I don't think it's too close at hand.

I'll send the little pet to you this Sunday 28th. She'll come with the basic minimum, I think the rest of her clothes can be sent on to you later, can't they?

She's been given a rag doll, you'll see how she fancies it, acts all maternal and caring, it's fascinated her.

My love, we have to keep our spirits up and be happy, we're near the final push. We have to prepare ourselves for the worst and give it our all, even our lives. It's already cost our people so much suffering and so many lives, that we have to give all for all. We can't achieve victory without sacrifices, can we? There are so many comrades committed.

My Darling Love, I want to have you with me, I miss everything about you, your caresses, kisses, our discussions, the lot. I love you, darling, remember I'm waiting for you.

Darling, I still have to tell you some things about child-care, we have to give her some coddling without letting her become spoilt. You have to be aware that her surroundings will seem strange to her at first, and you have to be understanding. She's a little poorly, she hasn't managed to shake off her intestinal infection, they're going to do some stool tests, and give her a chest examination.

Remember about her milk: 3 spoonfuls of milk, 1 of sugar, 1 of Nestlé's and $7\frac{1}{2}$ of boiled water. She eats anything, but not too much fat. She gets her orange juice at 9 a.m. She eats fruit (bananas, etc, in the afternoon). Look after her, my love, I feel my heart sink, but I'll be strong, my love.

It'd have been good if the little girl could have first gone to your mum, wouldn't it? Even though I prefer her to be with you.

I don't know how much longer this can last but, my love, I'm ready for anything and to sacrifice everything, even though it hurts. Write to me via this letter-bearer as communication will be difficult. Your letters overwhelm me so much, and I keep re-reading them. I'm sending you the photos and the tape recorder (without the lead that Ruth still has), you can pass them on to your relatives.

They didn't give me the poppet's birth certificate today; the solicitor's papers (to get the authorisation document for the visa) are ready.

Well, my life, what can I say. I love and wait for you. With all of my strength, energy, worries, I love you always. Kisses.

Hopefully, we'll be together the 26th February. The date for the 4th still stands, so long as I don't have to cancel later.

On 30 December, in the middle of the final preparations, serious security problems and imminent changes, Eugenia wrote another long letter to Javier, in which she included three pages of detailed instructions about Ana Patricia's diet and care.

My Darling Love,

I think of you so much and long to have you close by and to be able to talk to you, now more than ever.

I told you that I believed that at such a critical time it'd be unwise to move me on to a job I didn't know. It's really a different order of problems: the structures are undergoing changes, the working methods are appalling, there's a lack of knowledge as to how a leader should behave in practice, it's necessary to 'issue orders', also an ignorance of certain basic matters.

It seems vital to me that a leader knows how to lead and

135

everything about the work she directs. At times my spirits flag (which doesn't mean that I don't keep up continual efforts at comprehension, but there are some basic issues I don't have the hang of), it's not something I can manage to move along with all the speed demanded by the exigencies of the present moment. But if it falls to my lot, I'll put in all I can to make it a little better bit by bit. We're counterparts, Darling.

I saw Esteban today and it seems as though I'm going to be moved on, as someone's arriving from your region, so it's logical that he should take over. I'll tell you then where I end up.

Today a serious problem arose, they picked up two cousins who knew the workshops. You can imagine what a mess that makes of things at this point in time. We'll have to see how we get out of that one. The level of production worries me as it was already low.

I'll see you Sunday the 4th, my love, hopefully things won't alter. I'm waiting with both happiness and sadness for it hurts me deeply to be away from the little poppet too. I'm gathering strength to be equal to the task; hopefully so. Until now there's been no change; but I think they'll tell me tomorrow if they've moved me, which could change the arrangements. If I can't come, I'll send you the little poppet with my mum, okay?

I couldn't call you today because this problem had cropped up, and I only got away at seven in the evening, and I'd told you I'd call between five and six-thirty. I don't think there are any problems, but talk to my mum in the event of any emergency.

My love, what we've been waiting for fills us with inspiration, despite all the weak links, but we have to really launch ourselves forward.

My love, this is the decisive moment of all those we've so struggled on through. We have to give our all and make the greatest effort possible.

Right now so many of us are separated in order soon to be reunited in an atmosphere of proletarian freedom.

My Darling Love, remember I've always loved you, that each day I love you more, I've learnt so very much from you and remember too that most of all it was through you I discovered our people and learnt how to love. Thank you, Darling, I love you for ever.

My Darling Love, on the subject of the little poppet: remember lots of love and strictness, but don't hit her. There are things she still doesn't understand, that's true, but don't let her develop bad habits.

Today the doctor told me she needs a good laxative, as she has a bacterial infection and that it'll hurt, as she's very bloated. I'll take her on the 2nd, so that they can give her the treatment to control it.

One or two details that aren't 'exaggerations' and that you must manage to attend to:

– Wash her hands frequently, as she's very keen on the floor. And wash them before feeding and going to bed.

– See as far as possible she follows a routine with her mealtimes and bottle feeds so that she doesn't over-eat . . .

It's late now, I'm off to bed, and I'll carry on tomorrow, the 31st. I think of you a lot and I'll go to sleep thinking of you. Tomorrow you'll feel especially near to me.

At midnight on New Year's Eve, amid the sound of distant rockets, Eugenia celebrated the arrival of the New Year writing Javier a love letter filled with revolutionary fervour.

31 December '80/1 January '81

Midnight is striking, I can hear the sound of gunfire, and all my thoughts go out to you as the new year opens in the middle of our people's military struggle for their freedom, another year of struggle, hope and faith in victory announces itself. I love you always, in our people and in our daughter. I love you, Darling, it's been a year filled both with richness and with pain, in which our love has been affirmed. Do you remember we spent the last new year together? Today we're physically apart, but I know that in these moments we're more united than ever. All the love there could possibly be, in the poppet and in myself, is there for you. You've rendered us completely happy.

At that time I was working out my first contribution. I hope we'll measure up, to place our building block in the construction of a free and united country. I think of so many of those with whom we journeyed. We're now advancing into the hardest part, birth pains for a blissful and joyous rebirth.

Kisses and all of me for you, together with my struggles and worries of the present moment, king of kisses, we love you.

On 4 January 1981, Eugenia and Javier managed to arrange what was to be their last meeting. That day Eugenia also bade farewell to Ana Patricia, who remained in her father's care. Javier recalled:

In terms of the offensive, in the face of the intensifying war situation at that point, the separation from her husband and child was a pretty severe blow. We spent maybe two or two and a half hours together at a very precious time. Over there I still have a letter which expresses it. It was the last letter I wrote and it never reached her. For us it was as if we had to concentrate our entire relationship into that moment, because there was always the question of whether we would see one another again; the possibility that the way would narrow and we'd go forward to the revolution or to death.

On that occasion Eugenia was very emotional. I think there was something unusual about her, like a form of presentiment. Several times she repeated that this might be the last time we met. She insisted that if she was killed, her only wish was that we guaranteed her daughter would be brought up to be a fitting child of her people.

From then on she was effectively fully involved in the military struggle itself, at the General Staff at the Central Front, as a fully-fledged guerrilla at the war front. I think it was a very significant stage in her revolutionary career.

She'd say: 'Right, for the time being, this people who brought us together, who've nourished all our love, who've given such depth to our relationship, today need us to be apart.'

She'd say that it was the enemy who separated us. But that by opting for the people we had chosen to be apart.

The next day, Eugenia stayed up late to write her last letter to Javier:

My Darling Love:

It's January 5th, I want to talk a while with you, I feel a great need to, I'm swamped by a hundred thousand things I've wanted to say to you and words fall short.

My love, yesterday your visit was so brief, but you so filled me with emotion. I found you more handsome than before; there was something special about you. There's always a space to fill; we never become sated together.

My love, I love you for ever. Today I sense your presence in a strange way there in everything I do and in me, *I feel my love for you growing by leaps and bounds; I feel our love is something very solid that grows and advances, rapidly to the beat of the war.*

Darling, I love you more each time. You can imagine how

much I miss you and how it hurts, but that's the way it is. I don't have either you or the little poppet physically next to me; your absence hurts horribly. Coming here today and not finding the little girl, not hearing her laughter, her funny way of talking, hurts so much, Darling, but I gain strength from our people and from faith in what we're fighting for. I hope it'll be over soon, but that's something we can't foresee. Darling, I love you both. I believe the pain of our separation is small compared with that of our people; it's worth putting up with in order to forge ahead.

We have to give ourselves completely and I'm doing all I can.

Darling, yesterday went by and I was tense, that was why I couldn't tell or express to you how much I love you, but you know I carry the two of you very close to my heart.

Today it's already harder to communicate with you and I know you'll be busy. I'll take care to look after myself, but I'll always try to meet the standard set in paying tribute to so many comrades whose memory we cherish, and whose example we follow.

I'll make every effort to stay in touch, hopefully it'll be possible.

I was leaving on the 7th but today's the 5th and the enemy wiped us out at Sapo, so it's said. We don't know the score, so we'll have to see how things pan out. Now all those who arrived today can't move on because of it. It seems we'll stay put till the 8th. The enemy has smashed us. There are so many weak links and worrying factors, still there's no other way but ahead. Our number one weakness is a real headache but we have to press on, don't we?

I feel weak, without appetite, I've spent two days without eating, but today I managed to, thinking of you, because if I don't I can't give of my best; now I'm nauseous. I'll do all I can, remembering you.

There's a major collapse in the department where I work, there's no planning or organisation. Some of the memos are useless, some acceptable. It's a mess and everything has to be ready for the 7th for us to set up there. That side of things is above all practical, but maintaining control is very difficult. It remains to be seen if I can manage to sort it out. I go about in a state of permanent worry. I feel it's all in chaos, but I comfort myself thinking I'm not alone. At the moment it's all a shambles; we're left far behind in a good many ways. But as the saying goes, 'things fall into place along the way'.[1]

Give the little poppet a giant kiss and all my love, I love her so.

I saw her picture today and she's beautiful . . .

I'll look after myself and, if not, I'll still love you always. It's so crucial to make a revolutionary of the child; but I'm falling asleep. I sleep too little, another great worry. I'll try to get a grip on myself.

The patrol is very dangerous here, one has to go saying one's prayers through the manioc fields. I'll take care of myself the best I can. I passed the clothes on to Comrade T. Hopefully she'll send them on to you, there's still some stuff here, but they told me the bag was already heavy enough. The toys and more clothes were left behind. I'll give some to a friend, and a few extra, in case you can come and collect them yourself. She has all our documents and clothes, see.

Darling, I'll stop now in the hope that this gets to you. I love you for ever. An endless cuddle and a giant kiss. All I am and have is for you and the little girl, and I'll put into practice all you've taught me. I won't disappoint you.

Look after yourselves carefully there. We'll meet, hopefully it'll be soon, your absence cuts me to the quick. All of a sudden there's a lot of noise, I wonder what it is. Kisses, I love you. Hopefully, this'll reach you. I entrust the little girl to you; look after her, and don't let her eat earth and shit. If you can, write to me, or leave me a letter with your mother, all right? Kisses, I love you, Darling, for ever.

SWALK. I love you two totally.

'Eugenia saw my mother,' Ondina told me, 'for the last time on 10 January. They'd been pretty much apart, but throughout December and January they were very close.

'On 17 January my mother had a premonition. She said she felt very sad, that a depression had engulfed her, and that she'd been crying. That was the day Eugenia died. She died on the 17th.'

Eugenia stayed on in San Salvador working on the last details of her Service Section up until the general offensive began on 10 January. Ricardo said:

She received the specific order to present herself at the command post at the General Staff at the start of the offensive. On 10

---

[1] Literally, 'one packs one's bag while advancing' – translator

January she attempted to get there but couldn't. Given the chaos then prevailing in the country, the commander had to go on foot.

It's some 60 kilometres. A group of comrades travelled together weighed down with arms they'd failed to get through earlier. En route they got caught in a small skirmish. They didn't succeed in making the whole journey at night because they had to pass between a number of ORDEN bases. They had to lose a whole day camping out, pitched there without anyone seeing them, without food or anything, until they got to the site.

I remember her arriving on the 11th at about six p.m. Without the faintest chance of a rest, she went off immediately to sort out problems in her area of service, there in the outlying zone. She had to begin to assume instant responsibility.

She had left everything well-organised in the capital, but she had to tie up loose ends in the outlying districts, which was highly complex given all it involved. It was a question of different structures, different mechanisms and methods. There hadn't been any time to go and visit the city outskirts, but she at once began to work with the organisation to be able to guarantee security in all the developing conflict. She maintained her working rhythm there. In a short space of time, some three days, she managed to consolidate the whole of the area.

In addition, since we left behind one group of the General Staff, I had to leave her with the responsibility for the other group. Eugenia stayed in the General Staff, in charge of not only the supplies and all that went to make up the Service Section, but she also had to supervise the entire logistics of the security system, everything relating to matters of arms and munitions.

Following on from the first few days of the offensive, the Front came up against an unforeseen situation. We'd assumed that the highways would be kept closed and that any flow of supplies would be impracticable. However, our members came up against certain difficulties and couldn't effect the closure.

After they'd discussed a series of questions with the higher grade – and it was two a.m. on the 15th – I went to wake our comrade up. They gave her the critical mission to return at once to San Salvador and reorganise matters, starting from the point where a fresh situation had developed. She had to arrange this and organise a delivery of arms and munitions that had stayed in San Salvador and which were urgently needed in order for us to be able to carry forward the struggle.

Before all this occurred she'd already moved her general

quarters out into a gorge, where she had a whole battalion. We woke and gave her her mission in the middle of her night's sleep, explaining it to her. It didn't take her long to grasp what she had to do and there were no comebacks or complaints; at once she answered me: 'Don't worry, I'll go tomorrow.'

Eugenia's return to San Salvador was an extremely dangerous undertaking for her. As time was pressing, she had to take a truck out on to the freeway between Suchitoto and San Martín. Not a single car passed along there, not a truck, nothing. The road was under the continual vigilance of members of ORDEN armed by the army with G-3 weapons.

She succeeded in reaching the capital on the morning of the 15th without mishap. On the afternoon of the same day she sent the arms consignment, hidden in the chassis of a truck, for the Felipe Peña Front troops. The comrades entrusted with the handover returned in low spirits. The contact to whom they were to deliver the consignment hadn't materialised at the arranged hour.

No doubt this news also worried Eugenia, but she gave orders that the supplies mission should be repeated on the following day, the 16 January. The second attempt likewise failed, and Eugenia had to confront taking a decision which had subtle moral dimensions.

She had to bring about the completion of a logistic mission. She didn't have to do so personally, but she had to set it up and give orders for it to be accomplished. However, the heart of the problem was as follows: who was capable of delivering our arms and ammunition with the least delay? Once the task was done, the Front would have achieved a greater ability to advance further in the offensive as a whole.

Eugenia was in charge of the operation. They'd made two attempts to accomplish it without success. Our comrade decided to undertake the mission herself and here we come to the crux of the matter.

She controlled the situation well, bearing in mind its inherent danger and the importance to the Front of making a qualitative leap in advancing the war. There was also her duty as a leader to consider.

In the first place, she decided that she had to guarantee that the subalterns were undertaking the mission effectively. In the second place, she had to determine the reasons why the mission hadn't been accomplished in order to overcome any problems. It was on this mission that our comrade, together with three male comrades, fell into an ambush.

Detailed reconstruction of what happened is difficult, precisely because none of the comrades survived. From what it has been possible to reconstruct, they got through in the truck but weren't able to effect their contact. There they were in a difficult situation. They couldn't hang about on the highway, and they couldn't carry on to Suchitoto, because that was impossible, first because there was no way through and secondly because if they reached Suchitoto they'd be trapped there. Obviously, they had to return in order to straighten out arrangements. It was on their return journey that the enemy caught them.

On the afternoon of 17 January, Commander Isabel was performing two-way tests on her short-wave radio. She told me:-

We picked up the police wavelength. Sometimes there are crossed lines. They began to mention following a truck carrying arms. That they'd identified the occupants and had already turned around to follow them. They asked what the next procedure should be. 'You know what you've got to do,' said the other voice. 'We'll go ahead and block them off.'

We continued listening out of curiosity; we really didn't know what it was all about. We knew they were following a pick-up, that it was on the way to San Martín, that it was loaded with arms. By the end we knew they'd killed the occupants. At that time we didn't know who they were.

About three days later I was at another encampment and comrades arrived bringing the post. There was a meeting and there was a letter for the head of the General Staff. I took it and read it. It went: 'Dear Comrades: we're informing you that Eugenia and her other comrades have been killed.' I only got that far and felt utterly stunned. I returned to reading and re-reading it, believing it had to be another Eugenia. But it was our own comrade.

I went outside and started thinking that it was a tragedy, and how it would affect the organisation. I began to think of Javier, of my own boyfriend (to whom she was also close), and Ricardo, who was leader of the Front and probably didn't know.

The information comes through like that: you unfold a piece of paper, and the first thing I saw was that Comrade Eugenia was dead.

So I wrote a note to Ricardo explaining what had happened

and sent it to where he was. I arrived there myself a day later, and we didn't talk about it, we didn't even want to think of it, but we had to address ourselves to the problem. We wrote a letter to Javier and another to my boyfriend. Ricardo gave orders to obtain more detailed information, to verify what had taken place.

A mistake had occurred. The signal given by the contact waiting to meet them had failed to come through. Some paramilitaries had picked them out as unusual, and didn't even bother to detain them. They were machine-gunned. The enemy came disguised as a plainclothes patrol. They followed them from behind and called up another patrol. The second one came to cut them off, which they did. And then they shot them.

Ricardo summed up:

Eugenia was not someone to let herself be taken prisoner. She was very clear and certain on this point. Her decision about the terms of combat proved final.

Inevitably, her death was a heavy blow for the whole organisation. She was a member of the Revolutionary Council and, had she not died, she would have been elected on to the General Committee at the next meeting.

It was an enormously heavy blow for the Felipe Peña Front. We received a first notification of our comrade's absence on about the 19th. Then on the 22nd we received the confirmation that our comrades had been ambushed on the freeway between San Martín and Suchitoto. From then on, in memory of all the contributions made by our comrade, the command post of the General Staff was given the name 'Eugenia Encampment' in honour of her.

Within the context of the General Staff, Eugenia had made a major contribution, through her experience, the sureness of her political ideology, her party militancy as much as in her sense of mission and organisational ability. She had not only this rare organisational ability but also a capacity for military leadership. She made sure that orders were obeyed in a cooperative spirit. She had the ability to be able to issue the order and transmit the enthusiasm necessary for it to be complied with in the best possible way, with the fervour that lies at the heart of the revolutionary process.

Javier was present at the interview with Commander

Ricardo and gave me the definitive summary of the life and death of his wife and comrade:

> In the opinion of many, what caught their attention was that despite her fragile physical build, she never faltered on any of her military missions, either on long treks or at times of great physical exertion. Her moral strength, her revolutionary faith, a certain mysticism, made her overcome all physical debility. One could cite as an example the instance of that 60 kilometre march to join the Front.
>
> I think that Eugenia's life was exceptional. From the moment she opted for the revolution onwards, she was a comrade always in the process of development, who grew as a political leader, as a soldier, as a revolutionary, a proletarian, a mother and a wife. She never stopped developing in any of these directions. She never left off climbing higher and higher throughout her life as a revolutionary.
>
> I think Eugenia died in this fullness. Fully happy. Death merely bestows the crown of heroism upon her profoundly committed life, without reservations.
>
> She always said: 'They won't take me alive.'
>
> And I'd repeatedly told her that it doesn't always depend on the will of the individual but to a large extent on external circumstances, but she repeated: 'Circumstances don't matter to me. They won't take me alive.'

And they didn't take her alive.

Ellen Kuzwayo
Call Me Woman

Ellen Kuzwayo now lives in Soweto, the sprawling black township outside Johannesburg. But she grew up in the 1920s and 30s on her family's beautiful farm near Thaba 'Nchu in the Orange Free State. That land was forcibly 'purchased' by the South African Government in the 1970s, as part of its policy of removing so-called 'black spots' from areas allocated to whites.

The author writes about the women in her family, the girls she taught as a young woman, her colleagues in social and political life, and the women who shared political imprisonment with her in the 1970s.

Call Me Woman is destined to prove a classic of rediscovered women's history.

AUTOBIOGRAPHY/POLITICS
Paperback 0 7043 3936 6   £4.95
Hardcover 0 7043 2848 8   £9.95

Nawal el Sa'adawi
Memoirs from the Women's Prison

Translated by Marilyn Booth

Nawal el Sa'adawi is a leading Egyptian feminist sociologist, medical doctor, novelist and author of the classic on women in Islam, *The Hidden Face of Eve*.

Her career, as Director of Health Education in the Ministry of Health in Cairo, was a distinguished one. But in 1973 she was dismissed from her post as a consequence of her political writing and activities. Worse followed for in 1981 she was arrested for alleged 'crimes against the state', to be released only after the assassination of President Sadat.

This book is her powerful account of those months in gaol, describing both her own experiences and her encounters with other women prisoners, some of them political activists like herself, others veiled Islamic conservatives.

AUTOBIOGRAPHY/POLITICS   £3.95
ISBN: 0 7043 4002 X

Farida Karodia
Daughters of the Twilight

Meena, youngest daughter of an Indian father and 'Coloured' mother, grows up in a suffocating backwater in South Africa in the 1950s. These are the years when apartheid is under construction and Meena, quiet and introspective, watches her family respond in different ways as the pressure on their lives rapidly mounts. Yasmin, her sister, escapes to a private school, imitating the 'white' social world of riding lessons and 'coming-out' balls, which leaves her ill-prepared for the realities she must face; her father refuses to believe that 'the law' will really dispossess him of his home and business; and her mother desperately juggles the day-to-day needs of the family with ever-threatening poverty.

Yet even as the family is robbed of its home and livelihood, and Yasmin's cruel tragedy begins to cause the family to disintegrate, the overpowering impression is one of the strength, dignity and indomitable spirit of women in adversity.

FICTION
0 7043 4017 8   £3.95
Hardcover 0 7043 5007 6   £7.95

Shizuko Gō

Requiem

Translated by Geraldine Harcourt

'I must fulfil the responsibility of a survivor, on behalf of the dead who cannot speak for themselves; I must say what should be said and do what should be done'
Shizuko Gō

The year is 1945, Setsuko is a 16-year-old schoolgirl who writes letters to Japanese soldiers urging them to fight harder. Naomi is griefstricken because her father is in prison for opposing the war effort. Amid sickness, starvation and death, the two girls find comfort in friendship. They argue about patriotism, honour, democracy.

The firebombing of Yokohama brings destruction beyond imagination, and the end of their world.

Shizuko Gō herself survived the bombing of Yokohama. She waited nearly 30 years to write this immensely moving and powerful novel, which won the Akutagawa Prize, Japan's premier literary award, in 1973.

'Unforgettable and devastating, a book which the world needs'
Susan Griffin, author of *Woman and Nature*

'It contains the very important message that war is senseless and can bring no meaning to life' Petra Kelly, the Green Party, Federal Republic of Germany.

FICTION   £2.95
ISBN: 0 7043 3961 7

Jane Tapsubei Creider
**Two Lives:
My Spirit and I**

A unique insight into the vastly different worlds of Africa and
the West, and two fascinating autobiographies in one: the life of
the author, a Nandi woman now resident in Canada, and the life
of her spirit ancestor, Tapsubei, of whom the present Tapsubei
is a reincarnation.

Jane Tapsubei grew up one of the nomadic Nandi people in
colonial and post independence Kenya. As a child she learned
about her previous incarnation, a woman of great strength
who took to cattle raiding (traditionally something only men
could do) to win a better life. Inspired, the young Jane vows to
live up to this example – a vow which takes her to Nairobi, to
North America, and eventually to a career as artist and writer.

AUTOBIOGRAPHY/THIRD WORLD WOMEN'S STUDIES   £3.95
0 7043 4006 2